D1067732

OFF MY CHEST

OFF MY CHEST

by JIMMY BROWN

with Myron Cope

DOUBLEDAY & COMPANY, INC.

Garden City, New York

Library of Congress Catalog Card Number 64–22317

Printed in the United States of America

To KENNETH MOLLOY,
who was there when I needed him.

FOREWORD

In a figurative sense, the author of this book is two persons. As a fullback for the Cleveland Browns, Jimmy Brown's impact upon professional football has been loud and persistent. Off the field, however, he has carried himself with almost fierce reserve —with determined dignity that has prevented the public from knowing what manner of man the other Jimmy Brown is.

Although the performances of Brown the athlete almost defy description, syndicated columnist Red Smith provided a vivid glimpse of his style. "Once, after a blast of six or seven yards," he wrote, "Brown was the first to regain his feet. When he got back to the huddle he was blowing hard—but the inert figures of three Giants marked the trail where he had passed, like the bread-crumbs on the forest path of Hansel and Gretel. For mercurial speed, airy nimbleness and explosive violence in one package of undistilled evil, there is no other like Mr. Brown."

Perhaps the best measure of Jimmy Brown's "undistilled evil" is the fact that in 1963, only his seventh year of pro ball, he wiped out the all-time rushing record of 8280 yards that had taken Joe Perry thirteen years to accumulate. In the '63 season alone, Brown gained almost nineteen hundred yards—perhaps the most incredible sports statistic of our time. A panel of forty-two sportswriters covering National Football League games elected him Player of the Year.

But what of Jimmy Brown the man?

This book, we think, reveals him as a man of sensitivity—a reflective and forthright individual. Moreover, his story marks the first time a first-rank professional sports star has delivered an utterly candid account of his business while still at the peak of his career. Jimmy Brown has let the chips fall.

The result, we believe, is informative, entertaining, and frequently jolting.

MYRON COPE

CONTENTS

PART I

TWO MEN NAMED BROWN

CHAPTER 1

"Keep your mouth shut"

In the summer of 1957, when I first arrived in the Cleveland Browns' training camp in the town of Hiram, Ohio, a burly man named Lenny Ford took me aside and gave me a few words of advice.

"Rookie," he said to me, "if you want to get along here, listen to what I'm telling you."

"First," he said, "when you're running through plays in practice, always run twenty yards downfield. Don't just run through the hole and then jog a few steps and flip the ball back. The man doesn't like that. Run hard for twenty yards, even if you feel silly. He likes to see that."

"Secondly," Lenny Ford told me, "keep your mouth shut when he speaks to you. When he tells you how to run a play, run it the way he tells you. If you have an idea for improving the play, keep it to yourself. Suggestions make the man mad. If you're pretty sure you can make more ground by changing the play, change it in the *game*. Don't change it in practice. Run it your way in the game and hope it works, and if it does, don't say anything. Just make your yardage and act like it was a mistake."

Lenny was telling me to behave in a way that sounded kind of childish to me, but I wasn't about to mistake him for an idiot. He had been a famous All-American at Michigan and had since become a feared man in professional football. I kept listening. "Also," he went on, "don't start any conversations with the man. Don't *initiate* anything. You see something wrong, let it go. He does all the talking here."

The man who was being described by Lenny Ford was, of course, Paul Brown, our head coach. Working for Paul Brown in the ensuing years, I made a lot of money. I became the highest salaried player in the history of football. I'm paid more than fifty thousand dollars for a four-month season, and thanks in part to my football reputation I'm able to earn substantial money in business. So I suppose I should be able to say some nice things about Paul, and the truth is, I can. But I'm afraid I'll never rank as one of his leading admirers.

I don't think it can be seriously questioned that among all of America's coaches Paul Brown was far and away the genius of modern postwar football. This pale, tight-lipped little man was to jet-age football what Amos Alonzo Stagg and Pop Warner were to the game in another day. He was an original thinker, a man with ideas; but more than that, he was a painstaking organizer. He manipulated football players as he would chessmen (while encouraging little more self-expression than he would expect from chessmen). Doubling as general manager, he ran the front office as completely and sternly as he ran the ball game itself, attending to trivial details that could have been safely left to an office boy. Paul decided how we would travel, where we would stay, what we would eat, how much salary we would be offered, what type of promotional advertising the club would adopt, which players would be traded and for whom. He once hired his son Mike, who had played football at Dartmouth, as business manager. One of Mike's incidental duties was to announce what time the squad bus would depart for, say, the airport or the stadium.

Mike would step up and discharge his duty in a firm, clear voice. "The bus leaves at twelve-oh-five," he would say. And Paul, too, would step up and say, "The bus leaves at twelve-oh-five." Sometimes Paul would even take over for Mike before he'd finished the sentence. We always rooted for Mike to finish the announcement on his own.

The Cleveland Browns, one of the most astonishingly successful organizations in the history of commercial sports, nevertheless are a lasting memorial to Paul Brown. He was their first coach, and they were named for him. It does not do him justice to say that Brown *built* the Browns—he made them overnight. In his first year, 1946, they won the championship of the old outlaw league called the All-America Conference and for four years they were so clearly a great box-office draw that the National Football League was compelled, in 1950, to take them into their organization. Paul Brown's Browns promptly beat the pants off most of the teams that they played in the N.F.L., winning six straight division titles.

Men who played for Paul's 1955 team tell a story that goes miles toward describing the man. They had just come off the Los Angeles Coliseum field, where they had walloped the Rams in the N.F.L. championship game and were celebrating boisterously in their dressing room. The Rams, in their own dressing room next door, could hear their conquerers whooping it up. But suddenly Paul Brown climbed on a chair and spoke one sentence: "Act like this is old stuff." The room fell silent, and silent it remained.

The story of Jim Brown is in sizable part the story of Paul Brown, not only because I spent six years working for the man but also because in a sense all of us Browns *were* Paul Brown. Players became extensions of his personality, not only while on the field but in some ways while off it. They dressed as he would have them dress, and if they were prone to habits that he considered to be vices (smoking, drinking, cursing, women, etc., etc., etc.) they pursued them with the furtiveness of CIA agents. One day in the training room Bill Quinlan, a very tough defensive end, snuck a drag on the trainer's cigaret. Brown caught him in the act. "What are you trying to do, ruin my organization?" Brown raged. Quinlan, an earthy New England Irishman, told Brown what he could do with his organization. What Brown did with it, instead, was subtract Quinlan from it, trading him to Green Bay.

Each Friday Paul made a gesture toward democracy. He asked us if we had any suggestions. Sometimes we did. But as quarterback Milt Plum later said, "That's the last we heard of them." I quit offering suggestions many years ago.

We were a team of tradition, and part of that tradition was the knowledge that a man who went out of his way to make suggestions took his career in his hands. Before my time, two of Cleveland's better players were Edgar (Special Delivery) Jones, a back, and Jim Daniell, a tackle. Not long ago, Jones started the wheels turning in Daniell's memory when he recalled:

"We ran up a streak of twenty-nine games without a loss. Then we finally lost a game. Paul went wild. He would take each player aside individually, threaten to fire him and refuse to pay his fare home."

Jim Daniell listened to Jones's story and promptly topped it. "In 1946," Daniell said, "Paul appointed me captain of the team. He told me I was to be responsible for team morale. Well, we lost a game by one point at Los Angeles and he really took it out on the players. The players got those firing threats, so they came to me and protested. As head morale man I felt it was my duty to approach Paul. So I figured out a little speech. I told him how the boys were disgruntled by his continual criticism. 'If you nagged your wife every day at breakfast, lunch, and dinner I'm sure she'd leave you,' I told him. I thought I'd drawn a beautiful parallel. I thought my point was well taken. After all, I was supposed to be the head morale man. But my little speech just didn't work. Paul never spoke to me again, except when it was absolutely necessary for him to say something that had a bearing on our games."

In my own time under Paul, players privately referred to him as "that ——" (a seven-letter word that reflects on one's birth), and because he lacked hair they frequently enlarged the epithet to read "that baldheaded ——." I suspect that Paul, had he heard the words, might have taken them as a good sign that he was getting through to the players, but probably would have ordered them to vilify him in more decent language. Clean-mouthed myself, I called him Little Caesar. Silently, of course. As the other Brown in this opulently Brown little world, I kept my mouth shut.

For a considerable time I played the part of the big dumb fullback as well as I could, which is to say with a maximum of physical effort and a minimum of dialogue.

"Jim is a quiet fellow," the Cleveland *Plain Dealer* said of Jim Brown the rookie. "He seldom initiates conversation and he thinks before he answers."

After thinking, I usually came up with some kind of scintillating statement that endorsed God, country, and teamwork. Although Cleveland fans consistently received me with more warmth than any ballplayer has a right to expect, I can't help but suspect that they admired me as they would a large piece of sculptured stone or a strong draft horse. Bobby Mitchell, a wonderful halfback who somehow seemed unable to win Paul Brown's complete approval and finally was sent packing to score his touchdowns for the Washington Redskins, once summed up my public image when he said, "I go out to speak at banquets and I always hear, 'Jim Brown's really a big brute, isn't he?' "

That was me, Paul Brown's big brute.

This was never brought home to me so clearly as it was during a game with the New York Giants in 1959, my third year. It was then that my relationship with Paul hit a rock-bottom low from which it could never be restored.

The game in New York was our next-to-last of the season. On our first play from scrimmage, I bucked off tackle and was swarmed over. In the pileup, someone kicked me in the head. I suffered a loss of memory. I stayed in the game but I couldn't remember my assignments. I couldn't even remember having come into the stadium for the game. Milt Plum, our quarterback, had to explain my assignments to me in the huddle.

I carried the ball by instinct. Ring a bell and Pavlov's dog will salivate; hand a football to Jim Brown the beast and he will run with it. Even so, I killed a touchdown drive at the Giant forty by committing my first fumble of the season. Finally, late in the first quarter, Milt went to the sidelines and asked Paul to take me out.

The team doctor looked me over. I don't know what he told Paul, but I guess he told him he thought I'd be all right if I sat out the second quarter. In any case, at halftime I was lying on my back in the dressing room when Paul walked over to me. He did not say, "How do you feel?" He didn't ask me whether I thought I could play in the second half. He simply looked down at me and said: "Well, Triplett got hurt and he's back in there."

I didn't say a word. I just stared up at him and thought, "Well, dammit, do you think I'm trying to sit out? You think I'm trying to stay out of the game? All this time I've played for you and never missed any time–never been out with an injury–never wanted to sit on the bench and you know it."

I played the second half. I had regained my senses somewhat, but I was still in a sort of mental no-man's-land. I was dreamy out there. Sam Huff, the New York middle linebacker, who year after year has keyed on me with such slam-bang tackles that fans imagine we have a personal grudge against one another, was shocked to see me in the game.

"That guy's crazy," said Huff. "He should get you out of here."

The outcome did not exactly hinge on my presence in the lineup. The Giants were well on their way to a 48–7 victory. It's not often that a pro football team expresses concern for an opponent's well-being, but a number of Giant players wondered aloud that Paul would leave me in the game. They even took the trouble to help me to my feet after tackling me.

I am not saying that Paul Brown was callous and indifferent to the physical welfare of his players, who after all were important to him. He had consulted with the doctor about me. Moreover, my injury was the invisible kind—the kind that is not readily apparent to a coach absorbed in directing a total squad through a game. I did not especially resent Paul's leaving me in the game, but what I did resent, bitterly, was the remark he'd made at halftime: "Well, Triplett got hurt and he's back in there."

That kind of crack might have been called for if I'd had a history of injuries or been known as a chronic complainer. In that case, he might have had to needle me back into action. But the fact was that I had never sat out a game. In my three years playing for Paul, I had never missed a single minute of action because of an injury. To this day, I have never failed to be ready on Sunday; I have started every game on the schedule in my seven years as a pro. Sarcasm I needed from Paul? Like a hole in the head. Some may think that coaches have to treat players as Paul treated me that day, but I don't feel they do and never will.

As a consequence of Paul's words that day in New York, his big brute arrived at a policy-making decision. I would continue to run as hard as I could and say as little as I had to—but only in season. During the season, he paid my salary, I played his game. Winter, however, would be a time for speaking up, a time for needling Paul. A time for letting him know that I could be a difficult fellow, and hence a time for announcing to him that he would have to pay through the nose for my services. In short, if he regarded me as nothing more than a means to his end, a weapon for victory, I thought of him now as nothing more than a means to my end—more cash. I was willing to die for the dear old Browns, but I would take a lot of their banknotes with me.

I grew more talkative each winter, finally reaching the point of guerrilla warfare in 1962. From all directions on the banquet circuit, I peppered Paul. The teletypes of A.P. and U.P.I. hummed. I ventured the opinion that Paul might have made better use of Bobby Mitchell as a flanker rather than as a halfback. I told of instances when Cleveland players had wanted to go for first downs but were ordered by Paul to punt. I even crossed my fingers behind my back and declared that Paul had overworked me.

Paul fired back. "You know who's wounded if he doesn't carry the ball," he snapped. "Not this Brown." He was right. Chalk one up for Paul. But I was having fun.

Milt Plum had joined the good fight, publicly declaring that he was tired of Paul calling every play. Paul hit back with a barrage of statistics discrediting Milt's ability. Milt said the statistics lied. "The other players," he said, "could back me up on all this but I don't believe anyone will speak up." Shucks, I was willing.

"The players have the feeling they're playing under wraps all the time," I told my next banquet audience. "A little freedom would help." I gave Paul more lip than he had ever known from his employees, but once I signed my contract I clammed up.

During the football season, many sportswriters must have thought me a dull guy. They constantly wrote high praise of my performance and yet they must have said to one another, "This guy is lousy copy." And I was.

The resourceful sportswriter is one who hustles downstairs from the pressbox as soon as the game ends and burrows his way between the dressing-room lockers, sidestepping flung towels and hopping over benches to pry lively quotes from the cast of characters. Now is the time to corner them. They are either aglow from victory or very angry from defeat. Either way, they are apt to be quotable. But I was not.

I answered questions with as few words as possible—sometimes with only a shrug. Remember, I was billed as the club's star. It did not behoove me to stretch my status too far and become mouthy with the press. "Thanks," a reporter would say, meaning, "Thanks for nothing." He would then drift over to the circle of sportswriters gathered around Paul Brown, who as a rule was perfectly charming with the press.

One afternoon, just after we'd beaten St. Louis in eighty-six-degree heat that had sort of tuckered me out, a reporter said to Paul: "Did you ever use Jim Brown *more* at the beginning of a game than you did today?" Paul bristled and snapped, "No!" He was touchy about suggestions that he overworked me. "Well," said the reporter, "he carried the ball or was your pass receiver on twelve of the first thirteen plays." The implication was that if Paul's answer were true, he would at some time in the past have had to use me on thirteen of thirteen.

"When you've got a big gun, young man," Paul told the reporter icily, "you shoot it."

Moments later, he turned back to the reporter with a smile and assured him that he had meant no offense. Paul was careful with the press, even to the point of apologizing for a lapse in charm. He socialized with Cleveland reporters who covered our team. Under the circumstances, I had to be careful in my own way. I spoke at length to no writer unless I knew him to be the kind of craftsman who does not misquote.

On the ballfield, too, I remained silent, strictly observing Lenny Ford's advice while Lenny himself found it impossible to contain himself. Although Lenny had given me words of caution in my rookie year, he was an irrepressible rebel at heart. Several times he spoke up to Paul. Paul's concept of correct defensive play was unbending. He regarded unorthodox moves as dangerous, but occasionally it is the unorthodox move, wisely timed, that throws the quarterback for a fifteen-yard loss. One day Ford made such a move and threw an enemy quarterback for a ten-yard loss. Brown berated him when he trotted off the field. "Well, coach, you know, the quarterback's on his back," replied Lenny.

That kind of back talk never went over very well with Paul. Soon after, he traded Lenny.

Paul's own assistant coaches must have thought twice when tempted to differ with him. Howard Brinker, who coached both the defense and the offensive backfield, was more forward than anyone on the coaching staff when it came to suggesting tactics to Paul, but even Brinker had to go about it in a manner so devious as to be amusing. At halftime it was Howard's job to list our second-half plays on the blackboard. If I felt I could gain good yardage with a particular play in the second half, I would tell Howard on the way to the dressing room and he would then put the play on the board and launch into a long-winded explanation of why he felt the play would work. He would never simply tell Paul, "Jim thinks this play will work." He had to sell him on the play.

Howard Brinker always impressed me as an intelligent, even-tempered man. He was soft-spoken and absolutely loyal to Paul, never carping about him within earshot of players. One day, during a meeting prior to a practice session, Howard was lecturing on technique at the blackboard. I don't recall the exact technique that was under discussion, but Paul took issue with Howard's approach. Howard must have been in an uncharacteristically rebellious mood that day, for he stuck to his guns. Paul tried to interrupt him, but Howard doggedly ploughed ahead with his theme. Whereupon Paul turned red and barked, "Shut up!"

You could have heard a pin drop in that room. This was a real fine man up there, and there was not a player in the room who was not terribly embarrassed for him. Howard did shut up, and kept inside his belly the hurt that he felt. He continued absolutely loyal to Paul Brown. Perhaps he understood the man much better than I was ever able to.

I now find it in myself to speak my full piece in these pages because, very frankly, Paul Brown no longer is my boss. He ceased being my boss after the 1962 football season. Arthur

Modell, the young New York advertising and television executive who had purchased control of the club only a year earlier, received a good deal of sharp, you'll-be-sorry criticism for letting Brown leave and was labeled a front-office meddler. I felt, and said so at the time, that Modell had good reasons for his action. Four million dollars' worth of reasons. He put up that much money for the club and was brash enough to feel it entitled him to have a say in what went on around the place. Such thinking by an owner was completely foreign to Paul Brown.

Prior to Modell's arrival on the scene, the major stockholders in the club were wealthy Clevelanders–men who were big guns in steel, merchandising, broadcasting, and so forth. Nationwide Insurance, holding 30 percent of the stock, had a seat on the board. As illustrious as our owners were, Paul ran the shop solo. The owners were nice fellows who occasionally would show up at a banquet and shake my hand and pat me on the back, but so far as I know, they exerted no influence in the operation of the club. They got seats on the fifty-yard line. One had to admire Paul's independence.

He sat as absolute monarch in a spacious, nicely appointed office in Tower B of Cleveland Stadium. But then, Art Modell came to work one day.

The coexistence of Paul and Art began beautifully. Paul offered Art his office. Art said that's nice of you, Paul, I'll take it. Paul moved into a less distinctive office, but Art called for the decorators and had them make Paul comfortable. So far, so good.

Coexistence, however, was doomed.

Modell was not going to be one of those absentee owners so prevalent in big-league sports. He worked at his job. He showed up at practice every day to study his investment. But he did not, of course, let Paul Brown go merely to assert his authority. The Browns had lost their grip; they had not won a division championship since 1957, and Paul Brown, however great his brilliance in years past, was the major reason for the club's decline, it seemed to me.

It is my honest opinion that in his last five years as coach—five years in which we were an also-ran every season—every last one of those five squads, given its fair share of breaks, could have won the championship.

"Now Jimmy Brown thinks he's a coach," people will say. And some will say, "Paul Brown made him a great fullback and now he's criticizing the man."

Well, Jimmy Brown does not think Jimmy Brown is a coach, but after playing professional football for seven years, he presumes to know something about the game. He assumes that he is entitled to get a few things off his chest—to say, for example, what he knows of Paul Brown, if for no other reason than to enjoy the experience of being able to talk again. Paul Brown did not make him the fullback he is, whatever that may be, any more than Paul Brown created Adam and Eve.

The simple fact is that in professional football, coaches teach very little technique, especially to running backs. Paul composed little paragraphs on how to run with a football and made us copy them down, but I regarded this as nothing more than a ritual that was not to be taken seriously. In pro ball, a coach's main job is to make correct use of the material he has.

For the most part, Paul Brown used me correctly. Many sportswriters wrote that he used me too much—that he ran me so often that my legs would weary and I would fade before my time. Against Los Angeles in my rookie year I carried the ball thirty-one times for 237 yards, prompting Rams coach Sid Gillman to say, "If he carries the ball that much in many more games, he's got to wind up either punch drunk or a basket case." I didn't agree. Sometimes I felt that Paul called my plays when others would have fit the situation better, but I have always loved to run. Overworked? No.

Nor do I agree with those who say Paul Brown's strict

rules of discipline hastened his departure. "Now that there are two professional leagues in America and a third in Canada, and players have a choice of employers," we hear, "Paul Brown could not hope to continue bossing his men with an iron hand. Players today won't take that kind of stuff if they have an alternative."

That's nonsense. A good pro goes where the money is, and he is willing to work for it. Moreover, he wants to play in the toughest league to prove himself. Paul's discipline may have been irksome to many, but they had to put up with it for only a small part of the year. Besides, the discipline was sound. It molded Brown's players into a tough fighting unit and increased their chances of winning championship money.

His critics harped on the charge that his "messenger system"—his practice of calling every play by sending a new guard into the game—became outdated as opponents threw up cagey defenses that demanded alert, improvised thinking—independent thinking—from the quarterback. I believe this criticism has been vastly overemphasized. There is a measure of truth to it, as I shall explain later, but criticism of Paul's messenger system does not go to the heart of his latter-day troubles.

Paul's real trouble was that his dynasty collapsed under the weight of his own importance. He was the man who had written the book. He had out-organized the competition and he had put in the new and daring plays that electrified crowds and won millions of fans for professional football. But now, new coaches were coming along—Jim Lee Howell and then Allie Sherman in New York, Vince Lombardi in Green Bay, and a long string of others from coast to coast. The new coaches—and the old ones, too—recognized Brown's genius and were quick to borrow from him. They also wrote new plays of their own, but Brown evidently hated to borrow from *them*. When he did, it was with reluctance, almost with stealth, as though he were stealing cookies from a jar.

For example, we would be in the film room, viewing movies

of our latest game. The St. Louis Cardinals, let us say, would run a new play–one that had given us particular trouble. "Gee, that's a good play," you'd hear players remark to one another. A week or so would pass, and then Paul would show up one day and say: "Here's a play we're going to put in our offense."

The play would be the same one we'd seen the opposition use against us. But Paul never mentioned that it was. He would simply put the play on the blackboard and we would jot it into our playbooks. We were the honest forgers, never admitting to ourselves that we were copycats. At least we didn't admit it aloud. Our leader could not bring himself to confess to the very thievery that was popular and necessary throughout the league.

When defeats began coming his way with increasing frequency he responded with an irritability that multiplied his difficulties. He traded away first-rate talent (and helped build Green Bay into a champion) and showed thin skin when newspaper stories began to meet less and less with his approval. Frank Gibbons, who writes a saucy column in the Cleveland *Press*, particularly disturbed him, but there were others. It was not unknown for Paul to come into a squad meeting and denounce a newspaper article at great length.

"These guys are trying to ruin our football life," he'd say. "They're trying to put us out of business. Don't open your mouth more than is necessary to them. I'll protect you, you protect me." Heck, we didn't need that much protection. We'd say, "That writer was talking about Paul, he wasn't talking about us." A player learns to take a lot of newspaper stories lightly, but the press really got under Paul's skin in his last years as coach.

To fully appreciate how ridiculous Paul's monarchy sometimes appeared, one had to be in on the conclusion of a squad meeting. There we were, each player seated in his own little chair–his name printed on it. (This eliminated the waste of approximately thirty seconds that might be spent finding seats. It also served to notify Paul if a player was missing, for his name would fairly scream out from the empty chair.) Now, the meeting ended. But nobody would leave the room ahead of Paul. He strode to the door first—always. Then the players would arise and in the fashion of football teams charge out of the room to the field. But now and then, Paul would be struck by an afterthought as he passed through the door, and he would stop in his tracks. Beefy football players would pile up in the doorway like extras in a Mack Sennett comedy.

Worst of all, Paul Brown's players had the feeling at the end that he no longer was obsessed with winning the championship but merely with having a good season, one that did not disgrace his name. Perhaps they were wrong, but it seemed to them that their mission was merely to "look good." Morale was shot.

So Paul Brown moved from his coaching job to a vice-presidency—"vice-president of I-don't-know-what," as he described it. He had been the best of coaches. This change was tragic, for he could have avoided it had he been willing to compromise—to give an inch here and an inch there, to update his methods just a fraction to the times, to acknowledge that a clubowner does not pay four million dollars just to get a seat on the fifty-yard line. Paul had tremendous pride, and perhaps that is why he had been a great coach. But if he ever returns to professional football, I think he will have become pliable. Few men are the same after leaving what had looked like a lifetime job.

CHAPTER 2

The man who made me

If I were to pick one group of people that has puzzled me most in my lifetime, that group would be coaches. It's hard to know what to expect of them.

When I attended junior high school and then high school in Manhasset, Long Island, my coaches were strictly high-class gentlemen. I was a duly elected warlord of a roaming teen-age gang and was an indifferent student, yet my coaches saw potential in me and brought me along to the point where I became a senior class officer and an interested student. To my mind, a coach was a great guy. I went to Syracuse University thinking the coaching in college would be even better, if that was possible.

At Syracuse the coaches practically crushed my spirit and all but finished me as a football player. They had not given me an athletic scholarship at the beginning; I was therefore uninvited, and moreover was regarded as a potential troublemaker. For reasons that will be explained later in this book, the Syracuse people assumed that I would soon be chasing every white man's sister. I had to prove that I was interested in touchdowns, not white girls.

Was this the open mind of higher education? Was this the academic world of the enlightened North?

After a time, I proved that I not only had no interest in miscegenation but could score touchdowns as well, and then I was accepted. I grew to love Syracuse and to admire and respect the head coach, Ben Schwartzwalder. Later, I helped Schwartzie recruit the Negro Ernie Davis, my successor as a Syracuse All-American, and I have watched a stream of Negro athletes enroll at Syracuse. I owe Schwartzie my gratitude for having toughened my running style and gotten me ready for pro ball.

Anyhow, the coach who made me a successful professional fullback was not Paul Brown. He was Curly Lambeau. I played exactly one game for Lambeau.

He thought I was terrible. I, of course, thought his judgment left something to be desired. I still do.

That game was a very unhappy three hours. But whenever I make a bank deposit I say a silent thank-you to old Curly for what he did for me.

Curly coached the 1957 College All-Star squad, a collection of happy young horses gathered from around the country by the Chicago *Tribune*. I was one of them. In one sense, selection to the All-Star squad might not seem like a very welcome honor, for the *Tribune's* promotion department each year pits the All-Stars against the championship team of the National Football League, and the All-Stars almost always end up being rattled from one end of Soldier Field to the other. The prospect of having a leg or arm or a foot broken and seeing one's pro career jeopardized is clear and frightening. However, a place on the All-Star squad is worth the risk, not only because of the prestige involved but also because of substantial social rewards the players receive during the training period that precedes the game.

On a bright midsummer day I tooled into the All-Star camp in my spanking new convertible—a bright red job with white top and white trim—the biggest and best Pontiac that a downpayment from my bonus money and thirty-six months of time payments could buy. The All-Stars train on the Northwestern University campus in suburban Evanston and live in the college dormitories. It's a pretty campus, only a stone's throw from the Lake Michigan beach and a short drive down Michigan Avenue to the bright lights of the Loop. Best of all, there is a peculiar tradition of competition connected with the All-Star camp.

This competition is waged by the local girls. Across the years they have demonstrated a competitive spirit that All-Star players might have done well to copy on the field. Anyhow, I have never heard any of the players protest the fact that the competition is over themselves, the players.

The local girls—a pleasing mixture of Northwestern coeds and homegrown community products—are there waiting when the players arrive in camp. There follows a succession of house parties which, I imagine, have left a few players a little tired as game time approached. Various groups of girls vie to get the players to come to their parties. Because there are more girls than players, the players are in a position to press their advantage, and I have heard that one or two of them have been mean enough to do just that. In any event, each evening when the final squad meeting of the day is concluded, the All-Stars charge out of camp like stampeding cattle.

The hectic social pace in Evanston is a very traditional battle that has brought forth its share of stars among the girls—that is, those who do not fade into obscurity after a single season. When an All-Star player reports to the pro club that has drafted him he frequently is cornered by the veterans who themselves have played in an All-Star game and is asked about good times in Evanston. "And then there was this little one," the rookie will say, ticking off another name. "Oh, yes," a veteran will sigh, wistfully. "Yes, I remember her well. Still campaigning, huh?"

But I was talking about Curly Lambeau. Curly was sort of a puffy-looking man who walked around smiling all the time, as if he had just eaten a good meal. This was not the Curly Lambeau

I had read about. Arthur Daley of the New York *Times* has written of Curly's boyhood in Green Bay:

"In every neighborhood game he was the leader, not because he owned the ball but because authority came naturally to him. He happened to be one of those rare characters who was meant to be a boss, not an underling."

At the age of twenty-one Curly founded the Green Bay Packers and for decades afterward was one of the nation's more prominent coaches. He popularized the forward pass and turned out championship teams and acquired a reputation as a Simon Legree. He once fined a burly lineman five hundred dollars and ordered him to write out a check on the spot. The lineman did so but said:

"If you cash my check I'll kill you."

"It won't do you any good," Curly replied. "It would merely cost you another five hundred dollars."

So I imagine Curly Lambeau was a tough enough man in his time, but now he was out of pro ball and there was no pressure on him to beat the New York Giants in this All-Star game, for although everyone roots for the underdog All-Stars, almost nobody expects them to win.

We had a happy camp. Curly set a curfew for the players but it was honored more in the breach than in the observance. He didn't really even coach the team–he more or less conducted himself as an easy-to-please administrator, allowing his assistants to do most of the coaching. He seemed to be enjoying himself.

When an All-Star squad reports to camp, all the backs and ends want to be chosen for the offensive team, of course, so they can flash their best razzle-dazzle scoring form before the huge crowd and the millions who watch the game on network television. Sportswriters are a dime a dozen in the crowd, for the Football Writers Association of America holds it annual convention in Chicago at All-Star time. Altogether, the game is a fine showcase for the pro-to-be. However, when we went into our first squad meeting a number of players who had been offensive stars in college decided it would be wise to volunteer for defense.

Clarence Peaks, who later became a powerful running fullback for the Philadelphia Eagles, figured he'd play more if he raised his hand when the coaches called for defensive volunteers. Peaks anticipated correctly that Don Bosseler, now with Washington, would be the no. 1 fullback. (I myself was a halfback at the time and therefore not in competition with Peaks and Bosseler.) Lamar Lundy, a very good end from Purdue, had played in the Big Ten in the shadow of Michigan's All-American end, Ron Kramer, another man on our squad. When the coaches gave us our plays, Lundy immediately suspected that he would have a hard time beating out Kramer at offensive end.

One of the plays, you see, was designated by the coaches as "the Kramer end-around."

"Hmmm," said Lundy. "Guess I better volunteer for defense. Here we haven't even scrimmaged yet and they've got a play named for that guy."

I received a small shock myself. My opponent for the halfback job was Jon Arnett of Southern California. Another play in the book was "the Arnett pass."

Now I had beaten out Arnett in the All-American voting, but he'd missed a good part of his senior season because of an injury. He was a fast, flashy runner and highly popular on the Coast. Actually, there had been considerable speculation in Los Angeles newspapers as to whether the Los Angeles Rams would make Arnett or me their first choice in the league draft. The Rams had telephoned me a number of times and I fully expected them to pick me, but they chose Arnett. Apparently the All-Star coaches figured the Rams were right, for here was this "Arnett pass" in the playbook. I decided to stick to offense anyway and see if I could beat out Arnett.

At the beginning the coaches broke us up into groups for sprint races to test our speed. Arnett and Clarence Peaks and I and several others were in one group. Arnett jumped the gun, and the others, after taking a few half-hearted steps, quit running. Not me. I meant to win Arnett's job. I kept running and caught up with him and passed him at the finish line. The other players asked Otto Graham, one of Lambeau's assistants, if he was going to run the race over. "Nah," said Graham. "That's it. Arnett won it." I figured I was going to have trouble making that first team.

Somewhat to my surprise, I found myself on the first team on the second day of practice, as I recall, and settled back to enjoy my stay in Evanston. My first-string status did not turn out to be a permanent arrangement, but for the present I enjoyed being an All-Star. The only disconcerting note in our daily routine was a rather peculiar system of calisthenics administered by assistant coach Don Doll.

Doll's calisthenics looked like something out of yoga. He would have us stand there and wiggle our fingers for perhaps four or five minutes. Then we would spend a similar period moving our necks back and forth. Next we would exercise one leg. Altogether, Doll's calisthenics sessions were the oddest and longest I've ever experienced. He conducted them very systematically, almost with reverence. I found them dreadful. But never mind the calisthenics.

There were a number of interesting people on our squad worth mentioning. One was Jim Parker, an Ohio State tackle. Parker was a huge man, about 270 pounds, who walked knock-kneed and always wore a rather stupid-looking grin on his face. He looked just as jolly as could be, and simple. The players immediately sized him up as a butt for jokes and welcomed him enthusiastically into the card games that took place between practices and meetings. At the end of each day, Parker lumbered knock-kneed down to the Western Union office and wired fresh money to his wife. He was the biggest schemer I've known in football. Today, he plays offensive tackle for the Baltimore Colts like he plays cards. He lets opponents think he's going to make all kinds of mistakes, and then he blocks them into outer space. He still looks as jolly and naïve as he did when he was an All-Star. I think he's saved more money than any man in pro football.

Another amusing character in our All-Star camp was a little bug of a halfback from Oklahoma named Tommy McDonald. McDonald was so serious about wanting to play that you had to feel sorry for him, because you knew he wouldn't play, and yet you couldn't help laughing at the comedy in his predicament. He couldn't have weighed more than 170 pounds in his equipment, yet he was a running halfback. He was real go-go-go, the hardest working guy on the squad. During practice he'd purse his lips and run with that ball just as hard as he could, but then something terribly discouraging would happen—like the time he tried to run around Lamar Lundy's end.

Lundy, who stands six-feet-seven, did not tackle McDonald. He simply seized him under each armpit and lifted him off the ground and held him in the air. I almost expected him to tilt McDonald over his shoulder and burp him, but he merely held him in the air and looked at him as if to say: "Look here, little fellow, you can get in a peck of trouble frisking around out here with us boys." After that, nobody paid any attention to poor Tommy McDonald. He kept working hard, but it was as if he wasn't there.

I believe it was the day that Lamar Lundy held him in the air that Tommy decided he would never make pro football as a running back. He became, of course, one of pro football's finest flanker pass-catchers with the Philadelphia Eagles and acquired a reputation as an entertaining eccentric as well, but when I knew him in 1957 he was a grim little guy who sat out the All-Star game and told off Curly Lambeau when the game ended. Tommy is not exceptionally fast but he learned how to be tricky and he gives football every ounce of effort he possesses. Nobody makes fun of him anymore.

My favorite All-Star player was a quarterback from Notre Dame. Stanford's John Brodie was our first-string quarterback; behind him were Purdue's Len Dawson (who walked off the practice field one day, telling a coach, "I'm tired of standing around doing nothing"), and this curly-blond Notre Damer named Paul Hornung. Paul seemed not at all crushed by his second-fiddle status. He was loose. He and I hit it off at once and became close friends in Evanston.

Paul had a great sense of humor. Besides that, although he was a Kentuckian, he was not the least bit race-conscious. He was a born boulevardier whose tastes drew him irresistibly to the better night clubs where he enjoyed the company of bandleaders and showgirls. Everyone liked Paul, and though he often operated as a lone wolf, he in turn liked everyone. Years later, when N.F.L. Commissioner Pete Rozelle suspended Paul for the 1963 season after discovering that he had placed bets on his own team, a great many moralists were shocked that the public continued to adore Paul and was willing to furnish him with a profitable livelihood in banquet appearances. I suspect this was just one more bit of proof that all the world loves a lover.

Anyhow, as much as the game little girls of Evanston tried, they could not succeed in monopolizing Paul's time. He meant to turn Chicago inside-out. He soon established a friendship with an exotic dancer—that is to say, a stripper. Not an ordinary stripper but a topnotch attraction. Inasmuch as such entertainers in Chicago did not get off work until 5 A.M., the arrangement presented a certain tax on Paul's stamina. He was, however, up to the challenge, without being the least bit secretive about it.

He arrived for football practice one morning and said to one of the coaches, "What's the latest any All-Star player ever got in after curfew?" "That's not the kind of statistics we keep around here," the coach replied. "Well, whatever it was," Paul told him, "I've broken the record. I just this minute got in."

Possibly that achievement had something to do with the fact that the coaching staff did not plan a major role for Paul in the upcoming game.

For my own part, I had been doing my best in practice and had been running with the first-team backfield most of the time. And then–it was two days before the game, if I remember correctly–the coaches listed on the bulletin board the players who would run through the goalposts at game time and be introduced in the floodlights. Something like twenty-two men were listed. I was not among them.

I was dumfounded and angry. If I've given the impression that players don't take the All-Star game seriously, rest assured that is not the case.

I wanted badly to play; and because of the comparisons that had been made of Jon Arnett and me, I particularly wanted to beat him out of the first-string job. Apparently he felt I wasn't much competition for him. In the years since, I've been told by Los Angeles players that when Arnett reported to the Rams' camp after the All-Star game and was asked how good a runner I was, he replied, "Well, Brown's a pretty fair straight-ahead runner, but that's about all."

If the reader doesn't mind a little backbiting among us girls, I'll put in my two cents about Arnett: I've always felt that he was just about the most fortunate man in football. He was drafted by a club in his home territory, where he had immense popularity going for him in his college days, and received the benefit of press, radio, and TV coverage that had a tendency to go overboard. His popularity was, of course, understandable. He was not a showoff but he did have a showy running style–he had great balance that enabled him to wiggle all over the field. So he might run fifty yards and gain ten. This tended to excite people.

It is no fault of Arnett's that he is popular, but if you are another player being compared to Arnett you like the sportswriters to stick to the facts. Once, for example, a Los Angeles newspaperman compared Arnett to several other running backs —including me—and showed that Arnett had gained more yardage than any of us. I felt a little shortchanged because the yardage credited to Arnett had been added up from his rushing, his pass catches, his kickoff returns, and his punt returns. The figure credited to me included only my rushing. At that, I figured it was a satisfactory total for a guy who's only a pretty fair straight-ahead runner.

So Arnett started the All-Star game at the halfback position that I wanted. Curly Lambeau did not entirely exclude me from his plans. He assigned me to boot kickoffs and return New York's kickoffs. The gay dog Hornung was scheduled for a lot of action, too; he was to placekick extra points, if the opportunity arose.

The weather on the night of the game suited my spirits. Wet and windy. We won the toss and, with a show of great confidence in our offense, elected to kick off. Angry with Lambeau, I determined to boot the opening kickoff over the end zone, more or less to release my pent-up hostilities. I charged up to the ball, kicked it with all my might, and watched it foolishly skitter out of bounds. I had to kick over. This time my kick went straight and true. It was a short blooper that would have been good for a single over second base. As I trotted back to the bench I observed that Lambeau looked as if his dinner had suddenly given him acid indigestion.

He felt a little better when our team recovered a Giant fumble and went in for a quick touchdown, but Hornung quickly wiped the smile off Lambeau's face. Specialist Hornung dashed into the game and missed the extra point.

Now I kicked off again. And again I kicked out of bounds. Lambeau had seen enough of me. Into the game came Hornung, his role expanded to include kickoffs.

The Giants handled our team pretty much as expected and

held a 17–9 lead midway in the third quarter when Lambeau, desperate to get some kind of offense going, decided he couldn't be any worse off with Hornung and Brown in the backfield. In we went.

We had the ball on our own thirty-six and began moving it. Paul clapped me on the fanny and told me to run out for a pass. I caught it for a first down and Paul said, "That was fun. I may use you again, Crazy Legs." Moments later, he hit me with another pass for another first down. We were having a good time at last. The crowd was beginning to turn back from the hot-dog concessions and the exit gates.

We chunked away at the New York line for a while, and then Paul whipped another pass to me for a first down on the Giant twenty-four. After two plays failed to produce results, Paul said, "Let's show 'em that first-down pass play again, big boy."

I zigzagged into the secondary and shook off the defensive back. But the Giant line had given Paul a strong rush on the play and he had to hurry his throw. It fell five yards short.

Lambeau yanked us out of the game.

"Sonofagun, we were moving that ball pretty good," said Paul, as we slid down to the end of the bench to get as far from Lambeau as possible.

Later, Lambeau told Paul to go into the game, and Paul grumbled at him but went in and played a little. In the fourth quarter the Giants threw us for a safety, which meant we then had to kick to them. Probably as an expression of his disgust, Lambeau called on me to kick. I did so, but told him my heart wasn't in it. All told, it was an unhappy night. When Tommy McDonald told off Lambeau after the game, he said, "And those are Jimmy Brown's sentiments, too."

But that night Curly Lambeau made me.

You see, he shook me up. I was hurt inside. I knew all my friends and all the fans I'd made at Syracuse had watched the game on television, and I knew what they'd be saying. "Maybe he isn't the runner he was cracked up to be. He got on a squad that had all the cream and he didn't even get into a scrimmage play till the second half." The All-Star game is a big deal for a college guy. I was really mortified. I said to myself, "Maybe there *is* something wrong with me. Maybe Lambeau and his coaches were right. But I don't believe that, and I'm going to prove they were wrong."

If I'd played a lot in that All-Star game and had had a good night, or even a fair night, I probably would have stayed in Chicago that night and partied and eased into the Cleveland Browns' training camp at Hiram, Ohio, the next afternoon feeling satisfied with myself. That might have been disastrous. You can't begin to count the number of college stars who have failed to make a pro squad because they assumed they had it made. Players with all the necessary talent have been cut, and nobody will ever know they had the talent because they are selling insurance or teaching physical education. True, a few rookies who have collected big bonus money have made pro squads without going all out, but they often ride the bench a year or two, losing precious ground in the battle for annual salary raises. That could have happened to me. After all, there was a big, tough veteran named Ed Modzelewski waiting at Hiram to see that I didn't take his job.

I did not party in Chicago. Instead, I drove straight from Soldier Field to my dormitory room at Northwestern. I threw my bags into my car and drove all night, muttering darkly about Curly Lambeau. I arrived in Hiram at an early hour in the morning and was ready for practice. I needed no sleep. I was ready for work.

A few years later I ran into Paul Hornung, by now the rage of Green Bay, in an airport. We were making idle conversation when he said, "You know why Lambeau took you off the first team and made you ride the bench in that All-Star game?"

"Why was that?" I said.

"Well," said Paul, "you remember the time I told one of the coaches I'd just broken the record for coming in late?"

"How can I forget it?" I said.

"Well, the coaches figured you were out with me that time."

"Who, *me?*"

"Yep. That's what they thought. I figured you'd be sort of proud to be included," Paul said, and sauntered off to catch his plane, chuckling all the way.

It's possible that Curly Lambeau was not the man who made me. Maybe the man was Paul Hornung.

CHAPTER 3

Life with Paul

For one full season—my rookie season—I thought Paul Brown was a great guy. I heard other players griping about him all the time, but I couldn't understand their attitude. I thought he was a tremendous person.

Earlier, at the time he had drafted me, he had compared me in flattering terms to Marion Motley, the great fullback of the Cleveland Browns' early years. Paul told the press: "We hope Brown will be the next Marion Motley. Jimmy has a lot of the same attributes as Motley—size, speed, good running sense, and power. He should get the extra yard, and he should hurt opponents when they tackle him, just like Motley did."

Coming from pro football's top coach, those words were appreciated and gave me confidence. When I arrived in camp Paul greeted me with a smile and went out of his way to work with me. Far from being the grim man Lenny Ford warned me about, Paul dazzled me with compliments and solicitude.

He regularly made his players take written examinations to determine how well they knew their plays, and I had been in camp only a day or two when he scheduled an examination. Considerately, he asked me if I cared to take the exam. I said I'd like to, and when I finished the exam he said, "That's good, that's real good. You just got here but you know your assignments already. That's a real good sign."

He made sure I knew just what he expected of me. On the day of my first pro game, an exhibition against Detroit, Paul told me, "I'm not going to play you much tonight. You're not familiar with our system yet. I'll just put you out there to run two or three plays to get the feel of the game. Next week I'll play you a lot."

The next week we played Pittsburgh. Paul started me and gave me a good look. He ran me inside and outside. He had his quarterback throw to me. I caught three passes and ran well. ("It was shades of Marion Motley," wrote Chuck Heaton in the *Plain Dealer*.) In the third quarter, I broke through the middle of the Pittsburgh line, then shifted into high gear and raced through the converging defensive backs. I went forty-eight yards for a touchdown, showing Paul speed and maneuverability on the play. He pulled me out of the game and said: "Well, you're my fullback."

I felt wonderful. This was what I had missed in college—a quick, decisive vote of confidence. I said to myself, "Here's a coach who knows what makes his players tick. I'm going to like it here."

After my experience with Curly Lambeau in Chicago, I scrimmaged so hard in the Browns' practice sessions that I didn't even realize that a concerted effort was being made by our veterans to turn me into a flop. I never realized this till years later, when Ed (Big Mo) Modzelewski, the incumbent fullback, told a sportswriter: "Jim was fighting the law of the jungle. Let's face it, I had a lot of friends on the team. They'd try to hit Jim just a little harder than they normally would in practice. But he'd bust out of their arms and gradually you could see them gaining respect. You could see them thinking, 'Maybe he'll help us to a championship.' The writing was on the wall for me, so I became his no. 1 rooter. I felt like the guy who played behind Babe Ruth."

In a way, Big Mo was much bigger than I or, for that matter, perhaps Babe Ruth. The son of Polish immigrants, he had come out of the Pennsylvania coal fields and made a good life for himself in football. Yet even while his friends were trying to prevent me from eating his lunch, as the saying goes, Big Mo was going out of his way to help me. In practice, whenever I couldn't remember my assignment, Mo would whisper it to me with no coach the wiser. I might have looked like a dummy to Paul Brown many times had it not been for Mo. Today he operates a Cleveland restaurant called *Mo and Junior's.* The food is first-rate, the atmosphere sophisticated. But I doubt that Paul the Spartan would entirely approve of the place.

In the lounge there is a huge back-of-the-bar mural depicting the Browns in action. In the lower right-hand corner, Coach Paul kneels on the sideline. He is poised right over a real-life bottle of Scotch.

With Big Mo and Paul Brown encouraging me every step of the way, I had the kind of rookie year that no one dares hope for. I led the league in rushing with 942 yards. We won the Eastern Conference title. Although Detroit clobbered us, 59–14, in the championship game (both our quarterbacks were hurt), the season had been a happy and profitable one, and I had every reason to expect that I would always be happy working for Paul. I didn't realize at the time that Paul followed a pattern in his handling of men—a pattern in which at an almost predictable moment he would turn off his amiability as decisively as a plumber turns off the warm water with a twist of his wrench.

Given a rookie who had outstanding promise, Paul would flatter and cajole him. But after the rookie proved himself and got acclimated in his first season, he became little more than a spoke in the wheel. That may seem fair enough on the face of it. A pro is expected to do his job without having to be babied. Mo Modzelewski used to say, "Other coaches in the league shake your hand and kiss you when you score a touchdown, but what they're really saying is, 'Thanks for saving my job for another year.' Paul doesn't have to think that way—he runs the club and nobody's firing him. His attitude is, 'You're getting paid to score touchdowns.' " That was true. Moreover, the very fact that Paul so seldom complimented his players on a job well done made the few compliments he gave us all the more rewarding; one compliment from Paul Brown was worth ten from any other coach.

"Get yourself ready," Paul sometimes would say to me before a game. "I'm going to have to call on you a lot today." These words alone made me feel good. Coming from Paul, they constituted the personal touch. He seemed to be admitting that there was actually something *I* could do to help *him.* I knew there were times when he depended heavily on me, and when he uttered only so much as a veiled hint that this was so, I appreciated it. It's always been important to me that my coach have faith in me. The mere fact that Paul worked me so much in the games meant that he believed in me. I appreciated his faith in me and responded to it as best I could by running hard. Even the most indirect compliment from Paul affected his men.

Yet there is another side to the coin. In the atmosphere that Paul created, his players inevitably became robots. You played hard but you concerned yourself almost entirely with your own performance. "I've done *my* job," you told yourself. When a teammate scored a touchdown, you didn't go out of your way to hug him or pat him on the fanny. When the ball changed hands you went to the bench and sat there in silence. You cared, but the action on the field moved you to no demonstration of emotion. You were as close to being a mechanical man as a football player can get.

As the N.F.L. developed a balance of power that made every game a tough one, it became obvious that robots no longer would do. The Browns lacked spirit.

Paul's idea of creating spirit was to assemble his players at the opening of training camp and hit them with a speech that somehow had the tone of a warden telling a new inmate what he expects of him. I missed his speech my first year, having reported late from the All-Star game, but when I first heard it in 1958 Gordon Cobbledick of the Cleveland *Plain Dealer* was there and printed the following faithful account of it. Paul told us:

"We're going to be as good a football team as the class of people you are. We intend to have good people because they're the kind that win the big ones. If you're a drinker or a chaser you'll weaken the team and we don't want you.

"I'm talking to the veterans as well as the rookies here today. If you're an older player and have reached the point where you can't concentrate on what I have to say, maybe you've reached the point where you ought to be looking for other work.

"If you think about football only when you step on the field, we'll try to peddle you. You've got four and a half months of this ahead of you, and for four and a half months I expect football to be the biggest thing in your life, as it is in mine.

"In this game, more men fail mentally than physically.

"Maybe you've read or heard that there are four or five jobs open on this team. I want to tell you right now that that isn't true. There are thirty-five jobs open. They're going to be won by the men who convince me and the other coaches that they're best qualified to fill them.

"I like to think that the Cleveland Browns are somewhat different from the average professional football team. I want to see some exuberance in your play, some sign that you play for the sheer joy of licking somebody.

"We've been in business thirteen years. In eleven of them we've won division championships. In several others we've taken the whole pot. We're the Ben Hogans, the Joe Louises, the New York Yankees of our game and that's the way we aim to keep it.

"At home and on the road we stay together. On the nights before home games we go to a downtown hotel in Cleveland. We eat together, go to a movie as a group. It gives us a feeling of one-ness that helps to make us a team and not just a collection of thirty-five football players.

"I expect you to watch your language, your dress, your deportment, and especially I expect you to be careful of the company you keep. That pleasant guy who invites you to dinner may be a gambler. Probably he doesn't intend to offer you a bribe. Maybe he isn't even after information. But he wants to be seen with you in public. I'm telling you to avoid him.

"Here's a rule: In your rooms at 10, lights out at 10:30. Occasionally the coaches make a bed check. For the player who sneaks out after the bed check there's an automatic fine of $500. And it sticks. I have had to levy many fines for violations of many rules, and I have never rescinded one for good subsequent behavior or meritorious performance.

"Here in Hiram we eat three meals a day together. Sport shirts are approved, but I don't want to see any player in the dining room in a T-shirt. I expect civilized table manners and table talk. There have been people who failed to make this team simply because they were obnoxious to eat with.

"We're determined to have a team of men who are willing to pay the price of success in football, and the price is high. If you approach this as just another job, another means to a pay day, we don't want you.

"I want you to keep your wives out of football. Ask them not to talk football with other wives. I've seen it cause trouble.

"Before the season opens I'm going to have to tell some of you—many of you—that you won't make it. It's the part of my job that I like least, but when the time comes my good wishes will go with you. Now let's get to work."

Paul continued to deliver his speech year after year, continuing even while we were in decline to remind us that we were the Yankees of football. Also, he clung to certain rituals that had made his training camps famous. For one thing, we had to take an aptitude test that was much like those given high school and college students. Whether Paul ever switched an end to tackle because of, say, his math score, I really don't know. In any case, as the training progressed and we took on more and more plays, he measured our ability to absorb them by administering periodic written exams. These exams, together with the aptitude test, combined to give Paul a public image as a mental giant among coaches. Let's talk about those exams.

Whenever the exams were given, the players would be notified a day in advance and a list of plays on which they would be tested was furnished. They would then be assembled in street-clothes in a classroom, and Paul would deliver a few brief introductory remarks emphasizing the importance of the exam. We would listen straight-faced and gravely; not so much as a smirk could be found in the room. Paul would then depart, leaving his assistant coaches, who sat in the rear of the room, in charge. As Paul departed, small slips of paper would begin creeping from sleeves all over the room. These slips of paper were known as "gyp sheets." The extent of their use in Paul's celebrated examinations made the notorious West Point cribbing scandal look like child's play.

Among the first words of advice given to rookies by veterans were, "Get your gyp sheets made up." Long-sleeved shirts and sweaters were preferred dress on examination days, no matter how warm the weather. The gyp sheets, you see, were an absolute necessity, because Paul's examinations were impossible.

We had to diagram the plays, giving the assignment of every player on the team on every play. If you were a halfback, you had to know exactly what the tackle's assignment was, what the flanker's move was, and so forth from end to end. One mistake could very easily cause a succession of mistakes–if you put down the wrong assignment for one man, you very likely would give his assignment to another man, and by the time you finished the play your exam grade had plunged sickeningly. If that wasn't enough to confuse us, we also had to diagram several possible defenses against each play. In my six years under Paul Brown,

I did not know of one player capable of diagraming everybody's assignment.

Not even Frank Ryan, our quarterback, who was studying for a Ph.D. in mathematics, could score 100 percent without cheating. Lou Groza had played for Paul since the Browns were founded in 1946, and therefore might have been expected to know as much about Paul's system as anyone. Lou did have an advantage, it is true. He had a collection of gyp sheets to rival the card catalogue file in the public library.

The gyp sheets were tiny slips distributed at various points on one's person: under the sleeves, under the belt, just under the top of the socks, and perhaps inside the arch of the shoe. A player had to develop a small, fine handwriting to get down all the necessary information. However, he was not required to learn sleight-of-hand skills in order to safely ease his gyp sheet from hiding and tuck it back again. The reason he was not—and here's the delicious crowning touch in the entire farce—was that the assistant coaches in charge of the exam knew we were cheating and didn't care.

From time to time they would arise from their seats in the rear and walk up and down the aisles in a mock patrol. They would walk as loudly as possible to inform us of their approach. Whenever one of them came up on a player too quickly—that is, before the player had had time to tuck away his gyp sheet—the coach would considerately look the other way.

Now why, you may ask, did the coaches bother to patrol the aisles if they knew we were cheating, and why did we go to pains to conceal our gyp sheets from them?

The answer is that Paul's examinations had become an exercise in gamesmanship. Rules of honor had to be preserved. The coaches had to make a show of checking up on us and they never let on that they knew we cheated. The least we could do as gentlemen and scholars was refrain from being blatant.

Before going further, I should point out that not every man

who played for Paul Brown was a cheat. There were a few–either rookies or men sent to us in trades–who nobly rejected the advice that they draw up gyp sheets. This attitude was known in camp as "bucking the system."

Sadly, those who bucked the system made horrible exam scores, and Paul ordered his assistants to give them extra work on the practice field. Tom Wilson, traded to us by the Rams in 1962, had a commanding knowledge of football and took pride in it. Though a running back, he was a student of blocking and looked at a team with the over-all view of a coach. "I don't need a gyp sheet," he announced. "In Los Angeles we had basically the same system you guys have here." Wilson marched into the exam room and got mangled.

It seemed to me that Wilson's misfortune really pointed up how silly the exams were, for here was a guy who knew football inside-out yet couldn't lick that exam.

Now if there are any longtime Browns fans who cannot bring themselves to believe that the Cleveland organization, fabled for its ruthlessly scientific approach to the game, really spent hours at a time in these Alice-in-Wonderland shenanigans, let me specifically point out how fine and subtle were the rules of gamesmanship. Each player was expected to arrive at an honest appraisal of his own mentality and make just about the number of mistakes on his exam paper that Paul would expect of him. If you were stupid, you were expected by your teammates to admit you were stupid and not try to win a gold star for your forehead. On the other hand, it was quite all right if a guy like Chuck Noll, who had a high IQ and had played more than one position and consequently knew many blocking assignments, decided to cheat his way to a 100 percent paper. Perfect papers made Paul happy.

There were, of course, some players who didn't even know how to cheat well. I mean, the fact is that you have some guys playing rough, tough, first-rate football in the N.F.L. who are simply thick in the head. Even with the aid of gyp sheets, they'd somehow manage to score badly on the exams. Paul would look at their papers and frown and lecture the dunces sternly and then order extra work for them.

But it was his elation over the 100 percent papers that really puzzled us. We'd say to ourselves, "Is this guy for real? Does he really think anyone can know *every* assignment?"

I tried to view Paul's love of exams with detachment and make some kind of sense out of the whole business. I have only two explanations. One is that Paul simply was so wrapped up in this academic approach to football that he was blinded to what was going on. The other explanation is that he knew we cheated but didn't care, and had his reasons for not caring.

Did he, I've asked myself, give the exams simply to compel us to spend half the night drawing up gyp sheets and thereby learn something from that process alone? Was this his shrewd way of getting his men–particularly his younger players who had no adequate file of gyp sheets–to go over their plays? Maybe Paul felt that if a player learned just one thing, that single piece of knowledge was worth all the hours spent in preparing for the exam and then taking it. For example, maybe a lineman would notice that on the "60 Blocking" pattern, he got blocking help from a back. Was this Paul's goal? If it was, and if he knew all the time that we cheated and by his acquiescence encouraged it, how did this policy square with Paragraph One of his camp-opening speech: "We're going to be as good a football team as the class of people you are. We intend to have good people because they're the kind that win the big ones. . . ."

What's more, if Paul knew that we cheated, how does one explain the pleasure he displayed over the good papers and the irritation he showed over the bad ones? Was he play-acting, just as we were? I'll never know. I only know that I'm glad I've been able to throw away my file of gyp sheets. I get enough make-believe on TV.

Although Paul's coaching methods frequently were difficult to justify in my mind, I'd like to keep them in proper perspective. Great men, whatever the field they work in, often are peculiar men who go to excess. That's why they're great–they refuse to conform. They recognize no boundaries. Their mistakes are glaring and sometimes laughable, but their achievements are beyond the dreams of those who go by the book. To reduce this lesson to simple terms, consider the running back.

Some running backs make nervous wrecks of their coaches and fans by carrying the ball in the palm of one hand. Old John Henry Johnson, who has been fullbacking in the N.F.L. for ten years, once was described as a man who carries the ball "like a cake of wet soap." When he fumbles he is charged with carelessness. But to my way of thinking, there is no such thing as a careless fumble when you are talking about great running backs, and there is no such thing as a *wrong* way for them to carry a ball. If you're going to be a great runner you just can't tuck the ball away and fold yourself over it all the time. You can do that and be a good runner, a safe runner, but not a great runner. A great runner jumps and spins and changes directions and shifts the ball from hand to hand and takes terrible chances. He does things that make him look silly, just as great coaches do. Which brings me back to Paul Brown, whose greatness was indisputable until he himself became a conformist in the sense that he began to conform rigidly to every concept that Paul Brown had created.

Was Paul Brown a tyrant? Well, he was hard and, it seemed to me, unreasonable many times, but under his coaching the Cleveland Browns were the only team in football that worked a five-day week. We not only had Mondays off, but Tuesdays, too. Even on working days a player could safely plan a round of golf. "We'll be out on the field an hour and twenty minutes today," Paul would say. We would not work an hour and nineteen minutes or an hour and twenty-one minutes, but an hour and *twenty* minutes. Paul took orders from no source except the clock.

He carried his obsession with minutes and seconds to the point of mailing out preseason letters in which he informed his players that if they showed up one minute late for practice it would indicate bad attitude. All right, well and good. We benefited, because every minute Paul saved was a minute we'd have free for leisure. He was so tough that he would fine a player for being late for a pregame meal. Sometimes the culprit was a rookie, who perhaps would oversleep because his roommate had forgotten to wake him. The rookie would slip into the hotel dining room looking as scared as a man expecting fifty lashes. At such times I had to like Paul. He'd look at the rookie, then smile and say, "All right, eat your meal, but the next time that may cost you two hundred, you know."

Veterans, on the other hand, got no pardons. Bobby Mitchell and I almost knocked down an assistant coach one night as we raced headlong down a hotel corridor to reach our room before curfew. I once walked into a squad meeting five minutes late because the clock in the restaurant where I'd been having lunch was running slow. "That'll cost you fifty," said Paul as I took my seat. He gave me no opportunity to explain my tardiness, and I understood. I was paid more money than anyone on the team, and I got more publicity. Paul was making it clear that I would receive no special favors.

It's much more difficult for a pro football coach, even a Paul Brown, to dominate the lives of his players than it is for a college coach. Pro players, of course, do not live on a campus but go their way after practice. Still, compared to other teams in the league, puritan Paul's teams were known down through the years as milk and soft-drink teams. They were the opposite of, say, Buddy Parker's teams in Detroit and Pittsburgh. I've heard that Parker even buys beer for his Steelers after games.

The Steelers are renowned as men who have a lust for life. In fact, Dick Lasse, a fellow Syracuse alumnus whose flawless behavior makes Billy Graham look like a rake, told me after a short stay with the Steelers, "I had to get out of there. It was simply awful, the things that went on." Now I'm not saying that the Steelers are necessarily headed for hell when they die. As a matter of fact, when they're on the road they arrange to have clergymen conduct Sunday devotions in their hotel because churches cannot always be found close at hand. Nor am I saying that the Steelers' liberal ideas on training are necessarily wrong, for any veteran in the league will tell you that the Steelers hit like men carrying sledgehammers. I mean, they leave you bruised and battered. I've always called them the Gashouse Gang.

I doubt that anyone would say the Green Bay Packers, a partying crew of great stamina, suffered from dissipation. But I'm glad I played under Paul Brown's rules for living, because those are the ones I personally like. I don't smoke, nor do I drink, and I like to dress neatly. I would have to say that while a man possibly did not have as much fun playing for Cleveland as he might have had elsewhere, he saved more money.

Paul did not trail his men around town like a gumshoe and I'm sure he realized that some of them drank and smoked. His message was: "Don't let me catch you." And to a surprising degree, players obeyed his rules, because they knew that if he did catch them he would be merciless. Actually, he had to levy fewer fines than most coaches.

The one result of Paul's strict discipline that I found most curious of all was the fact that Cleveland teams seldom were troubled by player cliques. Why not? Because the players, fearing and in some cases heartily disliking the man, in a sense banded together for protection against him. All of us had something in common. We all knew that Caesar could reach down, pluck us out of the crowd, and throw us to the lions. There was safety in numbers, not in cliques.

As a footnote, I might add that Paul did play favorites in one respect. Offense was his baby. An offensive man was much better off than a defensive man. I suppose this traces to the fact that Paul called all the plays from the sideline and therefore had the vicarious feeling of being quarterback. Whatever the reason, it was easy to see in training scrimmages that defensive men got his goat. When the defense got a little rough and messed up the offense's plays, Paul would smirk at the defense and say: "All right, here's what we'll do if we want to score a touchdown against you." He would then kneel down in the huddle and with a flash of brilliance make up a new play. If the play worked, Paul would fairly strut. If it didn't work, he would look grumpy. You'd have thought the defense was a foreign force and not a part of Paul's payroll. Sometimes he'd take out his displeasure on Howard Brinker, the defensive coach, by hitting him with a few sharp remarks.

So why should I complain about Paul Brown? Man, I played offense.

CHAPTER 4

Close, but no cigar

The year 1958, my second season as a pro, is generally regarded as the time of the collapse of the Cleveland empire. Coming off our 1957 conference-winning year, we failed to repeat and from that time forward we were never better than second in the Eastern Conference. Yet I believe our '58 squad was a powerhouse —certainly the best offense I've ever been a part of.

We were deep in pass receivers. Ray Renfro, Pete Brewster, Lew Carpenter, Preston Carpenter, and I were experienced receivers. Such veterans as the great placekicker Lou Groza and the hard-blocking tackle Mike McCormack were men accustomed to picking up championship money. Jim Ray Smith, a third-year man, was a magnificent offensive lineman. What's more, we were blessed that year with a rush of new blood that seemed to come along at just the right moment.

Milt Plum, our quarterback from Penn State, had spent the previous season breaking in as successor to the retired Otto Graham and now was throwing the ball well. Gene Hickerson, who while at the University of Mississippi had been voted the outstanding lineman in the Southeastern Conference, reinforced our offensive line, where he has remained to this day. In addition we had a pretty fair rookie halfback out of the University of Illinois named Bobby Mitchell.

We opened the season in Los Angeles before seventy thousand fans and outscored the Rams, 30–27. We rolled through our next four games, scoring forty-five points against Pittsburgh, thirty-five against the Chicago Cardinals, twenty-seven in a rematch with Pittsburgh, and thirty-eight the second time around with the Cardinals. Our offense was so swift and powerful that we would actually joke and laugh in the huddle. "Well, now, we'll probably get about twenty this time," someone would say.

If Paul Brown told us to just run down the opposition's throat, we'd run down their throat. We *knew* we could move the ball. We had the kind of confidence that wins championships. We were averaging thirty-five points and 404 yards per game. So what happened to us?

Some of the experts trace the decline of the Browns to Otto Graham's retirement. Certainly Milt Plum was no Otto Graham, but who was? And after all, the teams we had to beat had no Otto Grahams either. I say we began to slip in the sixth game of the 1958 season, when Paul Brown banished to the doghouse a back who had torn the league apart for five games.

Bobby Mitchell had been positively brilliant almost from the day he put on a Cleveland uniform. He was an introverted kid —the opposite of the likably cocksure player he is today—but when you handed him a football or threw one to him he ran like a streak of lightning. He was Mr. Outside to my Mr. Inside, and nobody could anticipate the direction from which the Browns would strike.

Thanks to Bobby, defensive lines could not stack up for me like a pack of hungry wolves. Only the week before Bobby's strange demise, I'd scored four touchdowns against the Cardinals. In five games, I'd rushed for 815 yards, and Bobby, for 413. We were one-two in the list of the league's rushing leaders. Nobody was even close to us in yardage. We were having a ball.

Our sixth game was in Cleveland and seventy-eight thousand fans turned out to see us play the New York Giants. At halftime we led 17–7. In the third quarter, Bobby fumbled on two successive plays, though Pete Brewster recovered both fumbles before the Giants could. Still later, Bobby fumbled a third time but recovered the ball himself. Paul Brown, however, had had enough. He demoted Mitchell to the second team.

Paul's action was incredible to me. Okay, so we'd lost a game, and Mitchell had fumbled three times. But, prior to that game with the Giants, he had fumbled not once all season. I felt that Paul was taking away 30 percent of our offense. Throughout the league, Mitchell was a feared man. So effectively had he run that it took the next two games for the nearest man in the league's top ten rushers to overtake him.

At first, Paul replaced Bobby with Leroy Bolden. Bolden started against Detroit but after he gained a grand total of one yard on five carries, Paul put Mitchell into the game and was soon enraged to see Bobby, standing under a punt, misjudge his location and call for a fair catch on the 1-yard line instead of letting the ball go into the end zone. End of Bobby Mitchell. End of Cleveland offense.

Paul moved Lew Carpenter into Bobby's job. Lew, who previously had played flanker, end, and halfback, was a fine all-around player but one who simply did not have the breakaway speed to take advantage of every block and go all the way. Lacking the touchdown threat that Mitchell had given us, we became a scared team that was able to hang on in the race only because our defense got so tough that in the last half of the season no team was able to score more than fourteen points against it. Had Mitchell been playing, I think we could have scored at least fourteen against anyone.

Just imagine, here was a rookie back who in our first six games had rolled up five hundred yards rushing and thereafter was relegated to returning punts and kickoffs.

Why wasn't Mitchell playing? I have only the faintest notion.

It was in Washington's Griffith Stadium that Bobby first became a bench fixture. The field was muddy. After the game Paul told the press, "It just wasn't the type of going for a speedy back like Bobby Mitchell." A few days later, Paul looked ahead to our next game with Philadelphia and said: "Lew did a fine job in Washington, but we may want to take advantage of Bobby's speed if it's a fast track."

I got out of bed Sunday morning and anxiously went to the window. The sun was shining. At Cleveland Stadium the track was fast, but Lew Carpenter played halfback. Philadelphia ganged up on me and held me to sixty-six yards, my lowest yardage thus far in the season. Fortunately, Mitchell pulled us through by returning the opening kickoff ninety-eight yards for a touchdown and then returning a punt sixty-eight yards for another touchdown.

"His speed," Paul intoned, "is something special, and it may be that he's better when he's fresh." Lew Carpenter remained at halfback, and Bobby Mitchell remained fresh.

We went along that way, hanging onto first place by the skin of our teeth, right up to the season's final game in New York. If the Giants beat us, they'd be tied with us for first place. Sunday came up snowing. Rats. Goodbye to Bobby Mitchell's hopes of playing.

On the first play from scrimmage, I broke over tackle and went sixty-five yards for a touchdown, but then we settled down to our weekly Stone Age defensive battle. We lost, 13–10, and were forced to go back to New York the next week for a playoff game. Paul "indicated"–that was the word the newspapers used–that he would play Mitchell. He did not. The field was frozen fairly solid. "That was why I didn't use Mitchell as I had planned. Mitchell needs firm footing," Paul repeated for the umpteenth time. We lost, of course. In fact, we were shut out, 10–0. It was the third time that season the Giants had beaten us. When you have lost that many times to one team in a single season and been shut out in the bargain, you no longer are treated with respect, and sportswriters cease to describe your club as "vaunted." In short, the Browns had crashed.

Now with all modesty, I submit that Bobby Mitchell and I playing side by side—and not overlooking the fistful of pass receivers that Milt Plum had at his disposal in 1958—would have been shut out by no one. In any case, I couldn't buy Paul's professed reason for benching Mitchell.

"Jim Brown's a good mudder," Paul would say when pondering the elements. He repeated this description of me so often that I am known to this day—not only by the fans but by the players as well—as a guy who can plough through the mud. Although one wouldn't think so, players are influenced by what they read and hear. As a result, I'm known as a regular Man o' War when it comes to racing through the gunk. It's great to have the reputation, but it just doesn't happen to be true.

I slip in the mud and on frozen fields the same as anyone else. Just ask Leon Clarke. Ding-Dong, or Waffle Head as he was sometimes called, was one of my favorite teammates. No conformist was he. He ate raw steaks, collected machine guns, and usually had some kind of weird pet in tow, such as a monkey. (I am sure, however, that none of his unusual habits had anything to do with the fact that a thirty-eight-foot flagpole once fell off a building and landed on his head while he was sitting in his convertible sportscar.) Anyhow, Ding-Dong was doing a fine job at tight end one icy day in 1961 against the Bears. As for myself, I was doing a good imitation of Sonja Henie.

On one play, I took the ball and charged over tackle. Ding-Dong moved out ahead of me and was about to clear my path with a good shot at the linebacker. Just then, I slipped on the ice and crashed into Ding-Dong from the side. I knocked him out. He was hauled off to the bench where the doctor and trainer went to work trying to revive him. Just as Ding-Dong came to, I took off on an end run and skidded out of bounds beautifully with three Bears riding my back. You can guess where we landed.

Down for the count went Ding-Dong again. "Now I know how the other side feels," he said upon awakening, paying me the supreme tribute.

More to the point, I am saying that a wet or frozen field is murder for all runners. But Paul Brown in 1958 seemed to be repeatedly suggesting that it was worse for Bobby Mitchell because he was a fancy runner. That made a little sense to me, but did it also mean that all of a sudden Bobby Mitchell was nothing? That he belonged on the bench? If so, all fancy runners should be sent home when the weather turns damp and cold.

Bobby never did ask Paul exactly why he'd been benched. He simply sat by himself and suffered. He asked no questions, because one did not ask questions of Paul. In later years, when Paul got around to tolerating Bobby's swift and fancy running, we were never held scoreless (as we had been that costly day in New York). By then, however, it was too late, for team morale had plunged.

The Browns did not exactly fall apart, but our last four years under Paul were more frustrating to me than they would have been had we been a puny last-place team. We had material. We were always winners but never champions—the perennial bridesmaids. Close, but no cigar. All the while, Paul seemed to be living and coaching with one foot in the past. In practice sessions he constantly admonished us to emulate the men he had coached in the team's heyday—chiefly, Otto Graham and his fine receivers, Dante Lavelli, Mac Speedie, and Dub Jones.

If our ends dropped two or three passes in practice, or if our quarterbacks overthrew a couple of passes, Paul would say: "Otto used to come out for practice and say, 'Well, fellows, we're going to try to complete ten out of ten today.' And Lavelli and the others would get together and resolve to catch ten out of ten." It was Otto this and Otto that. If a quarterback did not throw quickly enough, he would be reminded that Otto used to anticipate the receiver's cut and would put the ball out there ahead of him.

Our receivers were urged by Paul to adopt a proper attitude –specifically, the attitude that Lavelli, Speedie, and Dub Jones had had. I'm sure these constant reminders irritated our players, for they weren't exactly slouches themselves. No doubt Paul meant to inspire them, but they were men living in their own time and they grew weary of ghosts from Paul's past.

Our defensive players, meanwhile, were chained to a system that had become outmoded. Each man in the defensive lineup had a specific assignment and was not to deviate from it. If he saw an opportunity to break up a play with an unorthodox move, he was to resist temptation and carry through with the defensive pattern. Paul recognized that this rigid approach would hurt at times, but it was his conviction that percentage was in his favor. Our opponents might chop away with small gains, Paul figured, but their chances of ripping off the long touchdown play would be small. "Don't put the defense in danger," he would bark at a player who had strayed from the pattern.

Norman Van Brocklin, who quarterbacked the Philadelphia Eagles to the championship before becoming head coach of the Minnesota Vikings, later told me: "Whenever I came up to the line of scrimmage I knew exactly what I'd see when I looked at the Cleveland defense. I liked it that way. It made my job easier."

Each man in our defense would be fixed in a prescribed posture. Defensive backs, for example, would crouch with their hands down just as Paul had taught them. And when the play began there would be no improvising. Consequently, the Giants, who lost only two out of eleven games to us in Paul's last five years as head coach, were able to beat us time and again with just a handful of plays.

The Giants would use perhaps three running plays, a screen pass, and a couple of other passes. They knew what our defense would do every game and stuck with the plays we couldn't handle.

Bobby Gaiters, a back who played briefly with the Giants, once told me, "Our guys figured that one of these days you guys would get wise and change your defense, but you never did." We were models of constancy.

Our paralyzed defense was a waste of good material that ran clear down through the ranks of benchwarmers. When Paul traded defensive end Bill Quinlan and substitute lineman Henry Jordan and Willie Davis to Green Bay, they promptly formed three-quarters of the Packers' up-front four and cut up championship money in 1960. Stashing fresh funds in the bank, Jordan remarked: "I thought I could have played for Paul Brown, but who am I to say? *He's* a genius."

Then Jordan added, "I'm pretty small. I play at 235. I have to play a slashing type of defense—move and let them guess where you're going. At Cleveland, Paul Brown has big guys and has them just stand there."

Our offense, meanwhile, was shackled by Paul's messenger system of sending in every play. While Milt Plum barked signals at the line of scrimmage, enemy defenses would change their alignments before his very eyes, but Milt could not "check off" and call a new play with an audible, for he was stuck with the play that Paul had sent in.

Nor could Milt take advantage of sound advice from our linemen. Those linemen knew how the defense was behaving, and sometimes they were practically positive that a certain play would work. "Jesus, we can run a four play this time," a guard would say. I could almost see a gaping hole opening up for me. But Paul would send in something else. Men would curse in the huddle.

Yet as I've said earlier, I believe that criticism of Paul's messenger system has been overdone. He was a brilliant play-caller, no doubt about it. There were many times when guys in the huddle would say, "He's out of his mind. This play can't possibly work here." And boom, the play would go for forty or fifty yards.

I vividly remember a midseason game in Baltimore in 1959. Paul went into the game nursing a grudge against Weeb Ewbank, the Colts' head coach, who once had worked for Paul. As nearly as anyone could guess, Paul was sore at Ewbank for having quit his staff. This explanation seemed too pat to me, because surely Paul recognized Ewbank's right to better himself. But whatever the reason, Paul had no love for Ewbank.

Like Paul, I had a special reason for wanting to beat the Colts. In my two previous years of pro ball, we had not had Baltimore on our schedule. Now, several Colts were saying that I was overrated and they would prove it. "I'm itching to get at that cat," said Big Daddy Lipscomb. My uniform number–32–was plastered all over the walls of the Colt dressing room and even in the shower stall. Real college psychology stuff. The Colts, the defending champions of the league and noted for their crushing defense, apparently had decided that they had to bury me as a point of pride.

Early in the second quarter, with the score tied 3–3, we had the ball on our own thirty-yard line. The situation was third down and eleven yards to go. Paul sent in his messenger with instructions to run a flip–that is, a quick pitchout to me. Nobody in our huddle thought we could make eleven yards with a flip in that situation. Besides, Milt Plum had been showing all the signs of having a big day with his passes.

Well, I took that flip and circled right end. Mike McCormack, our right tackle, moved out and slammed defensive end Gino Marchetti out of the play. Bill Howton, our right end, charged forward and removed linebacker Bill Pellington. Ray Renfro, our little flanker, skipped downfield and took care of cornerback Carl Taseff. The alley was wide open, but defensive backs Ray Brown and Milt Davis were racing from the opposite side of the field to close the alley. Brown hit me high, but I had a good head of steam up and shook him off. Only Davis was left, and now Bobby Mitchell scooted ahead of me and took Davis out of the play. The flip that nobody thought would work carried seventy perfect yards for a touchdown.

It touched off one of the biggest days I've ever had. I scored five touchdowns that day, and we beat the Colts, 38–31. Paul felt so good that he even treated himself to the satisfaction of brushing off Baltimore newspapermen when they tried to interview him after the game. John Steadman, sports editor of the Baltimore *News-Post,* wrote later: "Brown is a grown man but acts like a bitter little boy–It was the other Brown, the one who runs with the ball, who made life miserable for the Colts." This was not entirely true. Paul's messenger system had clicked beautifully that day. Unfortunately, this was not always the case.

Actually, it was my feeling to the end of Paul's days in Cleveland that if he had merely given his quarterback a slight amount of authority–if Paul had called, say, 90 percent of the plays instead of 100 percent–the messenger system would have been fine. But under his absolute hand, problems arose that were maddening.

For example, when there is one minute left on the clock and you're trying desperately to score, it does not sweeten your disposition to see messenger guards running in and out of the game, eating up valuable time. Your quarterback could be calling audible plays at the line of scrimmage and perhaps get in seven plays instead of four.

To show how silly our predicament could get, I might point out a situation that arose in a 1960 game against the Cardinals. Late in the first half, our Bernie Parrish intercepted a pass and returned it to the Cardinal nine-yard line. Only thirty seconds remained on the clock. We quickly called time out–our third and last available time out. Paul decided to try a pass. If it didn't click for a touchdown the incompletion would stop the clock and we'd still have time for a field goal from the nine. So Milt Plum threw and Gern Nagler caught the ball. But Nagler was hit in his tracks at the two-yard line. The clock kept running. John

Wooten, one of the messenger guards who alternated every play, was in the game. He knew that if he ran off the field and let the new messenger come in and call a huddle, time might run out before we could get off a play. But Wooten had been trained and conditioned, like a soldier under penalty of court-martial, to leave the field. He knew that we called no play on our own. Poor John was in a tizzy. He ran halfway off the field, then hesitated and came back a few steps, then stood there wondering just what the devil to do. Finally Paul's messenger came in. He brought with him no brilliant tactic–only the message that Plum was to give the ball to me and I was to try to ram two yards and cross the goal line.

I rammed across, all right. But the gun had gone off a split second before the ball was snapped. No touchdown.

Even when we were leading by three touchdowns with a minute or two left on the clock, Paul would call every play. The layman might assume that Paul's messenger system lifted a heavy load off the quarterback's shoulders, that it freed him from having to analyze enemy defenses and constantly search for the play that would work. The quarterback, one might suppose, had a rocking-chair job and had only to execute, never think. On the contrary, I felt sorry for Milt Plum because he had to concentrate harder than any quarterback in the league.

Other quarterbacks were able to relax by calling a couple of routine plays while they set themselves for a big play. For example, an end might tell his quarterback, "I think I can Z-out on that cornerback." So now the quarterback has to think of the play that will best give his end an opportunity to Z-out. He takes it easy for a play or two, setting up the big one. Perhaps the first two plays are deliberately designed to relax the defense against the Z-out. The quarterback is working calmly, deliberately. But Plum couldn't savor that luxury.

Plays came off the bench like machine-gun bullets. Paul calls for an 80 double-cross. Now Milt has got to recall everything he's been taught about the 80 double-cross. He's got to say: "Well, let's see. I've got double protection. My no. 1 receiver is my left end. I've got to watch the left safety because if he moves up that means there's going to be a pocket behind him." All of these factors, and many more, must race through Milt's mind. And as soon as he's thrown his pass, bingo, another play comes in, and he's got to start the whole mental process from scratch.

Milt was an even-tempered, level-headed man, but he became a nervous figure under Paul. When the offense bogged down, Paul would chew on Milt a little. Whenever Milt came off the field he had to report to Paul for a strategy conference. Milt got no letup. On the field he was always on edge. Today, Paul's admirers contend that Milt's uneven performance since being traded to Detroit in 1962 proves that Paul knew how to get the most out of him, but I can't agree.

As I see it, Milt was traded to a team of players who were more carefree and cliquish than the Browns. If Milt was to become their leader, it was necessary that he assert himself strongly. But he was a quiet, withdrawn person. Consequently, he had a lot of personality adjusting to do. On top of that, he suffered a lingering injury in an exhibition game and faded into the shadows in 1962.

The Cleveland Browns had been the ideal team for Milt to handle, if only Paul Brown had given him a pinch of freedom. The height of nonsense was reached in a game in which we were racing the clock, about twenty-five yards away from a touchdown, as I recall. Only a few seconds were left. We waited for the messenger. But lo and behold, no messenger came! Had Paul Brown actually forgotten? We were panic-stricken.

"Milt, you better call the play," someone said. "Time's running out." Milt didn't want to call the play. He was in anguish. He kept looking for the messenger, but still no messenger. Finally, Milt had no choice but to call the play.

Now I remind you, we needed considerable yardage for a

touchdown. A pass was in order. But Milt called for a flip to me. Why in the world a flip? Well, the flip was what Paul had called on the previous play. So now Milt said to himself, "I'd better play it safe and call the same play he gave me last time." In other words, Milt was only half-calling the play on his own. So conditioned had he become, he dreaded having to call a single play. Needless to say, we did not score.

By calling for the flip, Milt also was acting in the great man's image, for this was a play created by Paul—one he had introduced to football and seen popularized by many teams. It was simple but lightning-quick. Either the fullback or halfback could run it. At the snap of the ball the designated runner would break to the outside in a swift, sidewise gait. The quarterback would flip a fierce pitchout that would be taken on the dead run. I made a lot of yardage on that play, but the flip I remember most vividly was one that Paul did not intend me to run.

We had the ball on Washington's twenty-five-yard line. Into the game came Paul's messenger with orders for a flip to Mitchell. "Man, I'm bushed," Bobby said. "I don't know if I can run this play." "Well, look," I said. "All we have to do is switch positions and I'll run the play." So Bobby lined up at fullback and I at halfback. I took the flip, swept around my left end, and raced twenty-five yards for a touchdown.

Paul was pensively silent as Bobby and I trotted past him to the bench. We had countermanded his orders, or at the least, slightly revised them. This, we knew, was the kind of defiance that might send Paul rushing to market to negotiate a trade. Yet we had scored a touchdown, so perhaps Paul would overlook our crime. He uttered no comment that day, nor did we attempt to explain to him why we'd switched positions. But wait. On the following Wednesday we would have to sit through the films of the game. The Mitchell-Brown rebellion would be on the screen for all to see. Would Paul tolerate the sight of it a second time?

Assistant coach Eddie Ulinski assumed his customary role as

narrator of the films. He announced each play before it took place. "The next play will be 32 on 2." We watched 32 on 2, and continued to sweat through Ulinski's succeeding announcements. Finally the moment of truth arrived. Up on the screen, I trotted from the huddle to the halfback position, and Bobby settled into the fullback post. Ulinski started to speak but then stopped.

Only the whir of the projector could be heard in the room as I galloped silently to a touchdown. Paul watched without saying a word. The other coaches and players acted as though they hadn't seen the play. I'm sure that if I hadn't scored we'd have felt Paul's wrath, but as it was, he kept his feelings to himself throughout the film. But when the meeting ended he cornered one of our men and snapped, "You made a lousy block on that flip play."

Mitchell and I decided never to switch again. The next time we might not score.

Actually, my switch with Mitchell was neither the first nor the last time that I executed a play in a fashion other than that prescribed by Paul. But on the other occasions I was more subtle about it. Remember, when I was a rookie Lenny Ford had advised me: "If you're pretty sure you can make more ground by changing the play, change it in the *game*. Don't change it in practice. Run it your way in the game and hope it works, and if it does, don't say anything. Just make your yardage and act like it was a mistake."

Year after year, I found it necessary to alter a play on which I hit between my center and right guard. The way Paul designed the play, I would veer off to my right, then swing back to the left and hit into the line. In football terminology this movement was called a light bow. While I bowed, our line would open the hole by allowing the defensive guard to break through and run right into a trap. A halfback would block him silly when he charged into our backfield. The only trouble was that the defensive left tackle would slide over and cover the hole. The play wouldn't work. We had to get rid of that tackle.

I experimented and found that if I exaggerated my bow, arching deep to the right and giving the defensive tackle the impression that I was going to hit directly at him, he would have to hold his ground. Instead of moving over to block the hole, he would set himself to make contact with me. Meanwhile, my exaggerated bow would give our center time to slide down the line and put a solid block on that left tackle.

Throughout the last four years of Paul's reign, I ran the exaggerated bow while Paul prescribed a light bow. I just kept making my yardage and acting like it was a mistake.

I was by no means the first Cleveland Brown to deviate from Paul Brown's blueprints in order to gain yardage. Years after his 1954 club had won the N.F.L. championship, team captain Don Colo revealed that at least five offensive players had carefully plotted beforehand to ignore Paul's orders in order to win the championship game.

On the eve of the title game with Detroit, they met in a room in Cleveland's Carter Hotel. Colo did not name the men involved in the plot, but Otto Graham in all probability was one of them. As quarterback he was indispensable to the scheme.

"I don't know what motivated it [the players' plot]," said Colo later, "but Brown wasn't very conducive to changes in those days and they may have felt he wouldn't play it loose enough against Detroit."

Going into that 1954 title game, the Browns had lost three straight championship games and had lost to Detroit in the last regular season game only a week before. The players wanted the winners' purse badly, so they acted.

"Anyhow," said Colo, "during the meeting the players worked on a quick trap over the middle with Les Bingaman as the intended victim. Bingaman was big, but not very active. The idea involved blocking Bingaman the same direction the play was to go. They figured he would instinctively try to move the other way and take himself out of the way enough for Chet Hanulak to shoot through. Hanulak was quick and good at hitting up the middle. It was a trick play, one we hadn't shown before, and the doggone thing really worked good. I don't recall that it turned the tide, but it did produce a touchdown and a couple of other good gains."

The Browns walloped the Lions, 56–10. "Looking back," said Colo, who himself had chosen not to attend the secret pregame meeting, "it was basically a treasonous act."

Colo said the players expected to be blistered by Paul at training camp the following year, but Paul never mentioned their disobedience. "We never were shown the movies and it was just as though it hadn't happened," Colo recalled. Luckily, the treasonous act had gained yards.

As another who ran plays contrary to Paul's instructions, I thought it ridiculous to have to resort to underhanded methods in order to gain yardage, but what else could a man do when there was no rapport between him and his coach?

I had no relationship with Paul. I wanted to have a relationship with him, but his aloofness put him beyond approach. I did not want to be traded, because I liked living in Cleveland and in many ways liked playing for Paul. I loved to run, and he gave me the ball. I ran with it as well as I could, then showered and dressed and went on my way. I learned things on the field that Paul could not have learned from the sidelines, but I never dreamed of saying, "Coach, can I try this play a little differently?"

One phase, one period, in my non-relationship with Paul sticks in my memory. In 1958, my second season of pro ball, I set a league rushing record by gaining 1527 yards. I also had a crack at setting a new record for touchdowns. I needed one more to tie Steve Van Buren's record, two to break it. Four games remained on our schedule.

In the next three games we scored touchdowns four times on short-yardage plunges—but none of them was scored by me. Two of them had been scored from no more than a foot or two out.

Frank Aleksandrowicz

Pre-game introduction in Cleveland

1962 against the Baltimore Colts

A long run develops as tackle Mike McCormack clears the way. Quarterback Jim Ninowski, No. 15, watches. No. 81 (in white jersey) is Ordell Braase.

Malcolm W. Emmons

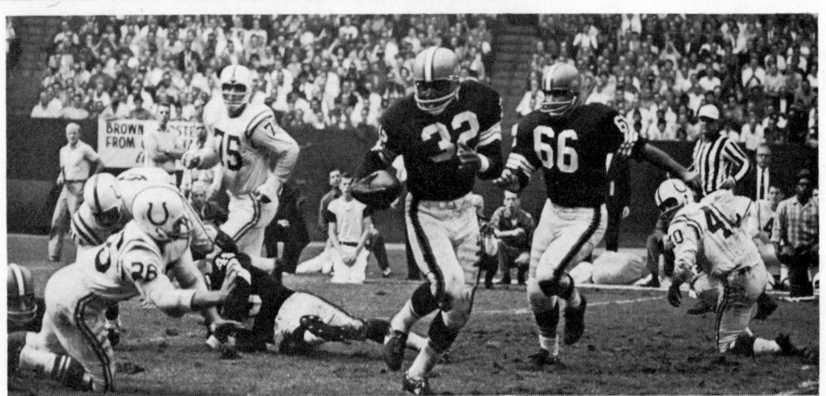

Malcolm W. Emmons

1962 against the Baltimore Colts

About to turn on speed for long gainer. No. 66, Jim Ray Smith, moves in fast to provide blocking.

Marty Reichenthal—Foto-Fin

2

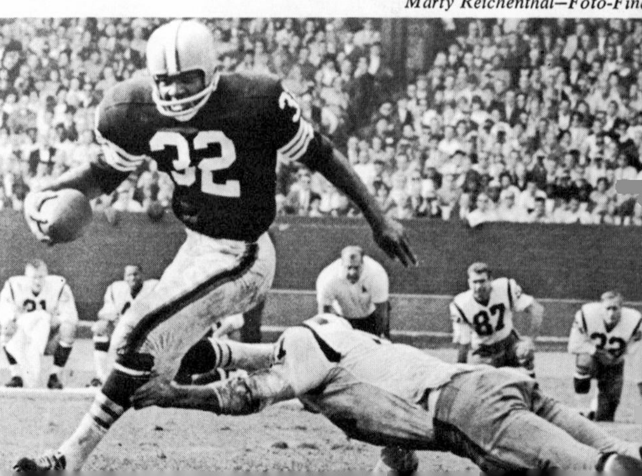

1962 against the Washington Redskins

Flying tackle by unidentified Washington Redskin misses its mark.

Frank Aleksandrowicz

1963 against the Los Angeles Rams

Breaking away for first down as tackle Dick Schafrath, No. 77, opens hole. Following the play is No. 13, Frank Ryan.

3

1963 against the Los Angeles Rams

Unidentified Cleveland player takes out No. 23, Bobby Smith, Los Angeles defensive back, to open "alley" to paydirt. Charlie Britt, No. 17, just misses tackle.

Frank Aleksandrowicz

1963
against the
Pittsburgh Steelers

Successful goal line leap.

Frank Aleksandrowicz

Frank Aleksandrow

1963
against the
Pittsburgh Steelers

Defensive man
George Tarasovic
misses tackle
that results in long gainer.

"How come Paul Brown didn't let *you* run those plays?" the boys down at the barbershop asked me. "I'm sure Paul isn't deliberately trying to prevent me from setting a record," I assured one and all.

Actually, the touchdown record was not a matter of major importance to me. I can honestly say that while I take some pride in breaking records I do not thrill to them. I can't even remember most of the records I've set; I have to go to the book to look them up. One day in 1961 a reporter charged into our dressing room after a game and offered me congratulations. "For what?" I said.

"For breaking your own rushing record, of course," he replied. "Didn't you hear the public address announcer tell the crowd you needed only fifteen more yards to break your own single-game record?"

"Oh, that must have been when they made the loud noise," I said. "I thought maybe the Steelers had come back to beat the Giants."

"Do you know what your old record was, Jim?" the reporter asked me.

"Can't say as I do. Something over two hundred yards, isn't it?"

The sportswriter must have thought I was pulling his leg, but I wasn't. Nor was I trying to be coy. I know that many fans are skeptical of athletes who say, "The record isn't important to me, it's winning that's important." Well, it's nice to set records and win, too, but in a way I almost dislike the thought of breaking a record. I hold more than a dozen records and as a result have been turned into a statistic. Newspaper and magazine articles dwell on my statistics and seldom show any insight into Jim Brown, the person. I find statistics boring. When I read about another athlete I want to learn what he's like and why he's able to do his job. I don't want to wade through a lot of junk that tells how many yards he gained and how many times he carried the ball and how many yards he averaged per carry.

Consequently, records do not thrill me and I was not upset when Paul gave the short-yardage scoring plays to others. But I could not help being amused when, after the matter had become the subject of public tongue-clucking, Paul addressed the squad and said, "I didn't realize that Jim was so close to a record."

Didn't Paul read the papers? The whole city of Cleveland knew I was on the verge of a record. But this intelligence had escaped the attention of the very man who would complain to the squad about unfavorable articles that appeared.

Well, in our final game, I managed to tie Van Buren's record by scoring on a short-yardage play that covered sixty-five yards. I couldn't have cared less.

Actually, the sort of thing that really disturbed me and others on the club was that, as the years went by, defeatism infected us. On Paul's instructions, our offense frequently avoided running at defensive men who were presumed to be tough. Playing against the Giants, for example, we were instructed to avoid outside linebacker Swede Svare. Paul said he was too tough. We were to avoid end Andy Robustelli. Also too tough. In other words, we were to be afraid of Svare and Robustelli.

I despised this approach, and I'm sure many of my teammates did. I've often found that opponents who have reputations as killers are in fact soft targets. In some cases, men who are over the hill remain stars because they're able to live off their reputations. Too many opponents steer clear of them. How are you going to know if a man is tough unless you give him a stiff test?

What's more, when you avoid him, when you make life easy for him, he certainly is going to become tougher by the minute. I agree with Giant coach Al Sherman's philosophy: run at the toughest man you can find. If you beat him, you beat his team.

Sherman's philosophy helped turn the Giants into champions.

In the meantime, whenever we played them we not only avoided their so-called tough men but often carried into the game a plan of attack that lacked daring–one that had been conceived in caution. The Browns-Giants games were the big ones; they drew big crowds. Instead of going into those games thinking we could knock the Giants off the field, we went in thinking, "Let's not get slaughtered in front of all these people." Paul had taken us into an era of play-it-safe.

I wondered if we would ever again come alive and act like Paul's old Cleveland teams had. Well, we did–for a brief period in 1962. That year, Brown hired a backfield coach named Blanton Collier. Our offense was all but thrown in the waste basket; modernization came to the Browns. We felt great. For a time we whipped everybody in sight.

But then, almost as abruptly as the 1958 season had turned sour with the benching of Bobby Mitchell, disquieting developments occurred and led to the junking of modernization. The '62 season was Paul's last chance to change. He chose not to. Blanton Collier, at first a dynamic addition to our club, retreated into the shadows. Dissension warped the squad. And finally, Paul Brown went.

His last year was, to my mind, the most puzzling of all.

CHAPTER 5

Comes the revolution

It's difficult to imagine two coaches who are less alike than Paul Brown and Blanton Collier. Paul was a coach made of wire; Blanton, on the other hand, wears like soft English woolens. Their meeting ground, I suppose, was that both made a science of coaching; both possessed a fastidious attention to detail.

When Paul brought Blanton to Cleveland in 1962, it was actually Blanton's second time around with the Browns. After the war he had helped Paul build his mightiest teams for eight years but then left the Browns to become head coach at the University of Kentucky. Now, in '62, he came back and immediately was a tonic to us.

In no way does Blanton fit the rugged, vinegarlike image of the pro football coach. Mild in appearance, he wears horn-rimmed glasses and has a round, kindly face. He is hard of hearing and frequently is forced to beg your pardon. Altogether, he looks like an algebra teacher, which is what he was at one time.

Blanton taught algebra in Paris, Kentucky, at a high school that had about five hundred pupils. He also coached the school's football and basketball teams, and during his sixteen years there won four football championships and seven basketball championships. Not being the pushy type, Blanton might very well have spent the rest of his career in Paris, Kentucky, had it not been for a world war that caused his path to cross Paul's.

During the war 2nd Class Petty Officer Blanton Collier's barracks windows at Great Lakes Naval Training Station overlooked the practice field where Lieutenant Paul Brown drilled the Great Lakes football squad. Soon Blanton took to hanging on the fence, taking notes. Paul became curious about him and had a talk with him. The result was that when Paul went to Cleveland in 1946 to form the Browns, Blanton went along as an assistant coach.

I know of no man who has played for Blanton who does not respect him. In a grim and sometimes brutal business, he has one quality that makes him stick out–sincerity. Blanton never jives anyone. If he wanted to he wouldn't know how.

Otto Graham credits Blanton with helping to make him the finest quarterback in the game. He drilled Otto in fundamentals and also set up the Cleveland pass defense. Paul assigned him to devise a system for grading player performance by reviewing films over the winter, and his first report was so enlightening that the study became an annual fixture and was expanded to include a painstaking evaluation of the success registered by each play. Painstaking work was right up Blanton's alley.

"Blanton Collier," Otto Graham once said, "is the greatest football mind in the country." Yet Blanton remained a nobody year after year. Finally he became a somebody when Kentucky picked him to be Bear Bryant's successor there, but during his eight years at Kentucky Blanton's teams barely won more games than they lost, and so his stay there ended. I don't profess to know what caused his troubles at Kentucky. Maybe he had no stomach for recruiting. Maybe the athletic program was at fault. Or maybe, as was later hinted by his successor, Charley Bradshaw, Blanton was too soft on his players.

Literally dozens of Kentucky players quit the squad soon after Bradshaw took over and began coaching with the fierceness of a drillmaster. "A great number of young 'uns have given up—given up any idea of playing football at this university," Bradshaw remarked to the press. In other words, he was saying that players had found life too easy under Blanton. Again, I wouldn't know, because I wasn't there. All I know is that when Blanton returned to the Browns, there were immediate and refreshing changes.

Our offense in recent years had become monotonous. Fans claimed they could sit up in the stands and predict the next play. Of course, we weren't all that predictable, but in my opinion we were definitely stereotyped. My own role was a bore. In the main, I was permitted to operate over an expanse of ground that extended from guard to guard. My off-tackle plays were not worth mentioning. Occasionally I ran outside on a flip or got there by bouncing off the middle of the line.

My philosophy as a fullback, it so happens, is that five eighty-yard runs in one game are not beyond reach. It can be done. In other words, I run with optimism. But it was hard to think big when you knew that your opponents could anticipate you. I had come to know the backsides of our two guards like the palm of my hand.

Suddenly, with Blanton's arrival in 1962, we became diversified. We had running backs in motion; we had double wing plays; we had a flood formation that inundated the enemy defense with pass receivers; we had a spread formation that moved both the fullback and halfback close to the line; we had our halfback running plays from fullback and our fullback running plays from halfback; our backfield blocking assignments were spelled out as never before.

Most pleasing to me, both running backs were now able to run anywhere on the field—inside and outside. I could sweep those ends free as a bird. No longer could defensive lines anticipate me. Wonderful.

I don't say that Blanton Collier put in our new offense. It certainly was a coincidence that the new offense came along at the same time as Blanton, but Paul was head coach and the head coach must be given credit for success and blame for failure because he is the man who ultimately shoulders responsibility for all strategy. He has got to say, "Go ahead," before any assistant can introduce a play.

With our new '62 offense we swept through every exhibition game on the schedule. Although it was Paul's custom to experiment with rookies in exhibitions, our new zest made us unbeatable. Sportswriters labeled us a comeback team and began picking us to win the championship.

We had lost some of our speed and striking power, it's true, because Paul earlier had traded Bobby Mitchell and a first draft choice to Washington in exchange for Ernie Davis, the Syracuse star who just before reporting fell victim to leukemia. Though we missed both Mitchell and Davis, we had acquired halfback Tom Wilson from Los Angeles, and throughout our exhibition victories Wilson looked like he would fill the bill. He did not possess great speed, but he was powerful and quick and could cut back with sharp execution. His only glaring error in his early weeks with the Browns was, as I noted earlier, that he thought he could take Paul's examinations without a gyp sheet.

Eighty-one thousand fans packed Cleveland Stadium for our league opener with the Giants. In recent years we'd become known as a team that usually flopped before big Cleveland turnouts, but this time we gave the fans a 17–7 victory. More than that, they saw something completely alien to our past performances. The back who carried the ball more than anyone else was not Jim Brown. He was the halfback, Tom Wilson.

Much as I like to run, I wasn't unhappy. Wilson's activity was a mark of our new diversification.

Too bad it didn't last.

Shortly after our victory over the Giants, an out-of-town newspaperman wrote a story hailing Blanton Collier as the man who had rejuvenated the Browns. Word circulated through the squad that one of Paul's friends had seen the story and mailed it to him. I cannot believe that the newspaper clipping–if it was indeed mailed to Paul–made him jealous of Blanton. Yet in the ensuing weeks, I could not help but wish that that article had never seen its way into print.

The Washington Redskins followed the Giants into our town. This time Tom Wilson carried the ball much less than he had in the opener. Paul kept me fairly busy, giving me the ball twenty times. We were still using our new stuff, but as he repeatedly passed over Wilson's plays I said to myself, "I've got the feeling our new offense is going out the window."

The Washington game turned into the most miserable day of my career. I committed two horrible mistakes.

In the first quarter I slanted off left tackle but met a solid wall. I glanced over my shoulder and saw quarterback Jim Ninowski and flipped a lateral. I've always been prone to lateral when trapped, because I believe in daring, improvised football, but this time I had no business putting that ball in the air, because I was in a bunched-up crowd. Washington's Jim Steffen picked off the lateral and ran thirty-nine yards for a touchdown. Washington took a 7–0 lead.

We slammed back to take the lead and in the fourth quarter were in front, 16–10. Whereupon I goofed again.

All we had to do to win was keep moving the ball for first downs and run out the clock. But I got too frisky. Paul sent in a play that called for me to flare out and take a screen pass. I caught it and saw daylight and ran twelve yards before two tacklers, charging shoulder to shoulder, cornered me. I had the first down and should have been satisfied. Instead I went for broke. I tried to split the two tacklers–I tried to charge head-first right through them. I fumbled and the Redskins recovered on their thirty-three-yard line.

Norm Snead, the young Washington quarterback, went to work competently. Five times he sent his running backs blasting into our line, moving the ball to midfield and setting us up for a pass. He hit Bobby Mitchell with a pass down the middle, and Bobby, fairly watering at the mouth with the prospect of beating Paul Brown, faked three men into the fifth row and ran for a touchdown. We lost, 17–16.

The defeat upset everyone on our team, but especially Paul. He had been beaten by those two old roommates, Mitchell and Brown. I sensed that he was very bitter toward me, and certainly I had to admit I'd played a rotten game. In his anger Paul threw our new offense into the ashcan.

Against Philadelphia the next week, we went back to the old Paul Brown formula. His trademark play–the flip–was back in business, even though we did not have a seasoned halfback on the squad who had the necessary speed to make the flip a threat. Against Philadelphia, moreover, it was Tom Wilson's turn to enter the doghouse.

A Philadelphia fumble gave us the ball on the Eagles' three-yard line in the first quarter, but we failed to score in four cracks at the line. Twice Wilson failed. In the second quarter he fumbled away the ball on our eighteen. Thereafter, he carried the ball only three times. The Eagles clobbered us, 35–7. The clomping sounds in our ears were those of sportswriters clambering off our bandwagon from coast to coast.

Wilson took the rap. The next week he rode the bench. Just as Paul Brown had abruptly abandoned Bobby Mitchell in 1958, he now found little use for Wilson the rest of the season. Mostly, Paul alternated rookie Ernie Green and Charley Scales at halfback. With no one man set at the position, things went from bad to worse.

Players were disgruntled. Practice sessions were run through in eerie silence. Blanton Collier, who at the beginning of the season had played a very vocal role in practices, now said little. He remained loyal to Paul, never opposing him to his face or behind his back, but we sensed a strained relationship between the two old colleagues. Blanton's fade into the background had the earmarks of a demotion.

We went into New York for our next-to-last game, hoping at least to beat out Pittsburgh for second place. The Giants, in first place, were beyond reach. They beat us that day, 17–13, as Paul had me chopping away inside with all the dazzling variety of a blacksmith. It was on the plane en route back to Cleveland that for the first time in history Paul Brown's employees decided it was time to beard the lion and thrash out their differences with him.

I was staring glumly out the window when defensive back Bernie Parrish slipped into the seat beside me. He said he was fed up with Paul's methods. I was, too. "His stereotyped approach is killing us," I said. Players were strolling up and down the aisle and drifting into our conversation. Soon we had a regular huddle going around my seat.

We decided that it was time to take action. A committee was appointed to seek a meeting with Paul and try to persuade him to open up our offense and perhaps make a few other changes that we thought were necessary if the Browns were ever to come back as a winner. Mike McCormack, our captain, and Bernie Parrish, Jim Ray Smith, and I were appointed to the committee. If we were in rebellion, our consciences were clear. We felt that we owed it to ourselves to make an honest effort to improve our club. We were simply going to state our grievances to Paul and request that he seriously consider their possible merits.

"Let's go back and talk to him right now," someone said.

"No," I replied. "This isn't the right time. Even if he listens to us he'll probably say we're upset because we just lost a game. He'll slough us off."

Someone suggested that the committee ask for a meeting at Paul's home. I was against that, too. "I've never been invited to his home," I said, "and I don't want to go there uninvited." Finally we agreed that we would wait until we reached San Fran-

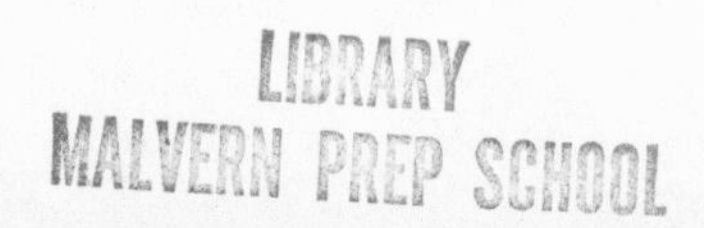

cisco the next week for our last game. We would seek out Paul in the hotel and ask for an audience there.

The meeting never came off. Somehow, Art Modell got wind of our plans. He said to me, "Maybe this isn't the right time for the meeting. Why don't you hold it off a while?"

Reading between the lines, I suppose Modell was saying, "Maybe this meeting won't be necessary." The handwriting was on the wall–Paul was on the way out.

Modell was well aware that for weeks there had been so much grumbling among the players that we had become a diseased organization almost beyond cure. Even after we abandoned our plan to meet with Paul and lay our cards on the table, some of us–I was one–told Modell that unless Paul agreed to change his coaching methods we would insist on being traded. If we weren't, we would quit. Modell was ready to move to protect his investment.

He waited till January to shock the nation with his announcement about Paul Brown, who coached the Browns for seventeen years. Paul's players weren't shocked. They had surmised that he would no longer be the coach and they were already hopefully wondering if Blanton Collier would be their next boss.

CHAPTER 6

Talking money

The paycheck has never been my sole reason for playing professional football. It is the prime reason I play but in itself it does not come close to explaining my love of the game.

When I report to preseason training camp each year in late July, I am not exactly delighted to begin work. Football is labor during the hot summer days. The game wasn't meant to be played in summer. But when September comes around and dabs of purple and gold begin to appear in the countryside and the air has a whiff of autumn in it, a man wakes up one morning and suddenly feels a sensation in his heart that for an instant takes the wind out of him and makes him take a deep breath. It is so with the veteran pro no less than with the college sophomore. You're just glad to be playing.

If I hadn't been good enough to make pro football, I'd be playing sandlot ball or touch-tackle with the kids in the backyard. Football is fun, and I can't imagine not participating. Beyond the fun, there is the feeling of pride that a man gets from excelling. Making the first team, making the Pro Bowl squad, playing for a title-winning club—all these are thrills that must be counted along with the money a player earns. Very few pros play only for a paycheck, and those who do are usually battered veterans aching from an accumulation of injuries.

Having stated my appreciation of the intangibles, let me say that I like money. The more I see of it, the *more* I like it. Club-owners love football, but they are in it to make money. As a player, I want as large a share of the profits as is reasonably possible. In order to get my share I learned early to be hard-nosed when facing Paul Brown across the bargaining table.

As general manager of the Browns, Paul negotiated all player salaries. Being also a stockholder, he could not have been expected to dish out the club's money with reckless generosity. He held a 17 percent interest in the club and in addition to his salary reportedly drew a bonus based on net profits. Such a bonus arrangement may not have actually existed, but it is certain Paul owned part of the club. So it was not surprising that at contract time he was a shrewd adversary—a man who deftly strove to take charge of the conversation and dominate it to its conclusion. While I resolved not to be swayed by his negotiating skill, I nevertheless had to admire it.

So far as I know, Paul paid his players fairly. When I say that, I must add that I don't know how much he paid other players, but I seldom heard them complain. It's possible that players were underpaid and ashamed to make it known to their teammates, but in any case, all of the Browns heeded the advice that Paul gave them when they signed. "Let's keep this figure in confidence," he would say. "Otherwise, it only causes trouble on the squad."

Throughout professional sports, of course, there is an unwritten rule that salaries remain a secret known only to the player and front office. Tony Kubek, the New York Yankee shortstop, got in dutch with his front office in 1963 for having publicly stated that players only hurt themselves by keeping their salaries secret. He pointed out that Moose Skowron for years received less money than Andy Carey, though Skowron was clearly more valuable to the club. Carey simply was the better bargainer.

A football player, unaware of his teammates' salaries, has no reliable measuring stick for deciding how much money to ask. It is said that if players knew their club's salary scale, they would become jealous of one another and dissension would set in. I do not flatly reject such thinking, because it is true that football is very much a game of teamwork and some athletes are prone to girlish jealousies that can be disastrous to the club. Yet, I suspect that if salaries became common knowledge it would give players new incentive that would more than compensate for ruffled feelings. Give a guy a yardstick and he will go out and try to have a big year so he can say, "Well, I'm the best man at my position now. I know how much money I'm worth and I'll get it." By the same token, the player who has a poor year will know how much money he deserves.

As matters stand today, many players have only a vague idea of their worth, and when they enter the front office to talk contract they sometimes begin to question their own judgment. "Maybe I'm out of line," they say to themselves. Maybe they are, maybe they're not, but the general manager has the upper hand because he alone knows how far the player must go to be out of line.

For all of Paul Brown's stern ways, he did not browbeat or rage at players during contract talks. He received them courteously and then went about dominating the conversation. Then again, he might depart from form, as in the case of Walt Michaels.

Michaels had given Paul ten years as a linebacker, but Paul's interest in him apparently had waned. They were unable to agree on salary by long-distance telephone, so Michaels decided to travel to Cleveland in hopes of settling the matter face to face. Paul granted him an audience in the company of his entire coaching staff. Under such circumstances, Michaels was uneasy talking money and got nowhere. He retired and went into coaching.

When it served Paul's purpose to review a player's statistics he would produce a batch of statistics. At other times, he might attack differently. Although the Browns were a prosperous corporation, Paul found it possible to brood about the club's ability—or inability—to pay. "Well," he'd say, "we made good money playing in Detroit last year, but we don't play in Detroit this year. We'll miss that money." Nickel logic, I called it.

Paul also liked to steer the contract talks away from brass tacks by bringing up names of other players and discussing them, though not their salaries. This backyard-fence gossip made players uncomfortable. They didn't really want to hear it. They wanted to get down to their own case.

Over the years, I developed some rather unorthodox methods of countering Paul's negotiating techniques and proceeded to the highest salary in the history of pro football—more than fifty thousand dollars. In the beginning, however, I was not particularly money-conscious.

In the fall of 1956, as my college career neared an end at Syracuse, I had no idea that I would ever play for Cleveland. The Browns were the only team in the league that did not send me a feeler. The Rams and 49ers had spoken to me on the phone, and the interest they showed caused me to assume I'd wind up on the West Coast. On November 26 the N.F.L. clubowners and coaches met in Philadelphia to conduct the first five rounds of their annual draft. They met at that early date because they wanted to beat the Canadian league to the top college players. The American Football League had not yet come into existence.

At the time, the feature of the league draft was the "bonus choice," which rotated from club to club each year. It was Green Bay's turn this time, and the Packers chose Paul Hornung, the guy whom Curly Lambeau was to find so little use for in the following summer's All-Star game. Then the various clubs began picking their no. 1 draftees.

Los Angeles, picking first, disregarded me in favor of the L.A. hometown star, halfback Jon Arnett of Southern California. Then San Francisco, the other club that had taken the trouble to telephone me, also decided in favor of hometown talent and chose quarterback John Brodie of Stanford. I was clearly no big shot in the eyes of the talent scouts, and the next developments were to underscore that fact.

Cleveland, Pittsburgh, and Green Bay—each with identical won-lost records in the N.F.L. standings—stood in line behind San Francisco in the draft proceedings. They held a "flip-off" to determine which of them would draft next. A representative of each club flipped a coin. The rule was odd man wins. The Browns and Steelers each flipped a tail, and the Packers flipped a head. The Packers chose Ron Kramer, the All-American Michigan end. (Coach Liz Blackbourn, by grabbing the likes of Hornung and Kramer in a single day, was doing a great job of stocking Green Bay for its eventual rise to power under Vince Lombardi.)

The Browns and Steelers tossed a coin for the next pick. Both clubs had their eye on the same player. Honesty compels me to report that the apple of their eye was not me. Purdue quarterback Len Dawson was the man both clubs wanted. The Steelers won the toss. Paul Brown was disappointed because since Otto Graham's retirement a year earlier he was still looking for a quarterback. Failing to get Dawson, he settled for me. He freely admitted he would have preferred Dawson.

So it was by the purest chance that I landed with Cleveland and commenced to be Paul Brown's big brute. The Steelers, meanwhile, were blasted by Pittsburgh *Press* football writer Pat Livingston, who the day after the draft wrote:

"The Steeler draft selections pointed up the wide difference of opinion between the team's coaches [then headed by Walt Kiesling] and Pittsburgh's pro football fans. . . . Bitter disappointment greeted the selection of quarterback Len Dawson of Purdue and tackles Bill Michael of Ohio State and Don Owens of Mississippi Southern."

Livingston went on to write that Steelers should have drafted me and Tommy McDonald. (Tommy didn't go till the third round.) With all due modesty, it seems obvious that subsequent events, both in Cleveland and in Tommy McDonald's Philadelphia stamping grounds, have made Livingston look like a pretty sharp talent scout. Don Owens is a first-string defensive tackle for St. Louis, but Len Dawson and Bill Michael have long since disappeared from the N.F.L. scene. Dawson rode the bench for three years in Pittsburgh. Then Paul Brown got him in a trade, but he rode the bench for two years in Cleveland and finally went over to the A.F.L. Quarterbacking the Dallas Texans, he promptly won the A.F.L.'s Most Valuable Player Award, and his admirers have contended that he never got a fair chance in the N.F.L. They may be right, who knows? All I know is that if it hadn't been for Len Dawson, I wouldn't be playing for Cleveland. Pittsburgh might have picked me ahead of Bill Michael and Don Owens, though one can't be sure.

After Paul Brown drafted me he dispatched Dick Gallagher, his line coach and talent scout, to visit me at Syracuse. We were getting ready to play Texas Christian in the Cotton Bowl on New Year's Day. I found Gallagher a gracious gentleman, but I told him I was not ready to talk money. I'd already discussed my pro future with an attorney named Kenneth Molloy, one of my best friends. Molloy, a kindly but astute man, had taken an interest in me during my high school days in Manhasset, Long Island, and had encouraged me throughout my college career. He had tremendous faith in my ability and was convinced I could make the Browns cough up a nice chunk of money.

"Don't sign anything now," Molloy advised me. "You'll have a big day in the Cotton Bowl and then you'll be in a position to ask for good money." I wasn't as certain as Molloy that I'd have a big day in the Cotton Bowl, but I had to follow any advice this man gave me. He'd always had my best interests at heart.

Just before the Cotton Bowl game, Dick Gallagher visited me in my hotel room and pressed me to talk money and sign, but I said no. Had I signed, of course, I would have technically become a professional and been ineligible to play in the Bowl. But no one would have known. It's a common practice for pro clubs to sign players before they've used up their college eligibility. The contract is tucked away in a safe, and once the player has played his last college game the pro club announces that he has just signed. The deception is harmless. I didn't object to it. Sometimes it enables a scout to get a mention in the newspapers by dashing onto the field at the finish of a bowl game and pretending to sign his man between the goalposts.

We lost to Texas Christian University in the Cotton Bowl but we made it close–28–27–and I scored three touchdowns and kicked three extra points. Now Kenneth Molloy invited Dick Gallagher to sit down with us in his law office in Manhasset.

I'd heard salaries discussed by other college draftees and felt that I'd be fortunate to get a ten-thousand-dollar salary. In those days there were no A.F.L. millionaire clubowners to drive up the N.F.L.'s bids. The Canadian league helped us a little–but not nearly as much as the A.F.L. has in recent years. Anyhow, I felt that my first concern was to make the Cleveland club and prove my worth before demanding substantial money.

Kenneth Molloy was more practical. He's a dapper little white-haired man who wears a bow tie and speaks at a snappy clip. His law practice is lucrative. He invited Dick Gallagher and me into his law library and listened patiently while Gallagher began the sparring, telling us the salaries that various rookies and even established stars were being paid.

"Nine thousand dollars is the highest we've ever gone for a rookie," said Gallagher.

"Well," replied Molloy, "we can get twenty-five thousand dollars from Vancouver." In point of fact, the Canadians had assured us they would top any N.F.L. offer. They had not discussed specific figures but they had seemed to be very big-hearted men, so Molloy felt justified in picking the twenty-five-thousand-dollar figure out of the air. Why not? "Why should we start with you people for nine?" he asked Gallagher.

"Canadian football won't be good for Jimmy," Gallagher countered. "He'd have to go two ways, offense and defense. Also, the weather's very cold up there."

"Nevertheless," Molloy answered, "I've investigated the pro football situation a little and I think fifteen thousand dollars would be just about right. Jimmy will be making a sacrifice, but he'd like to play in Cleveland and I'd like him to play there myself."

Gallagher said that we were demanding an awful lot of money. But Molloy stuck to the figure, so Gallagher finally asked to be excused from the room so that he could phone Paul Brown and discuss our price. After speaking to Paul, he returned and said, "I'm sorry, but we can't go that high. We can come up somewhat, but we can't go to fifteen thousand dollars."

"If you don't mind," said Molloy, "I'd like to speak to Paul Brown myself."

Molloy phoned Paul and told him: "I'm very happy that you're interested in Jimmy, Mr. Brown. You have a fine organization. In fact, if I had a son playing football, you'd be the man I'd want him to play under." Molloy paused a moment, then added, "However, you are asking Jimmy to make a big sacrifice, and I cannot admire you for asking him to make such a sacrifice."

"Let me talk to Dick Gallagher again," said Paul. When Paul finished speaking to Gallagher, Gallagher hung up and told us in a lighthearted friendly manner that we were trying to commit highway robbery and that the Browns could not submit to it. Molloy insisted they submit, whereupon Gallagher finally said: "We might be able to pay twelve thousand dollars and throw in a three-thousand-dollar bonus for signing."

Molloy agreed. Although I had gotten my fifteen thousand

dollars, there was a strategy behind Cleveland's proposal to pay three thousand dollars of it as bonus money.

If I had an unimpressive rookie season, Paul Brown would be able to negotiate my next contract on the basis that I had been paid a twelve-thousand-dollar salary—not a fifteen-thousand-dollar salary. If he cut my pay he could cut it to, say, ten thousand instead of thirteen thousand dollars.

As matters worked out, I had a big rookie year, leading the league in rushing with 942 yards. I scored ten touchdowns and I felt that I had earned my fifteen thousand dollars. "That was the worst deal I've ever made," Kenneth Molloy says today.

When I went in to talk second-year contract with Paul, he had a surprise in store for me. I did not have Kenneth Molloy with me this time, because I had decided it was time I started learning to travel alone. I'd decided I rated a three-thousand-dollar raise that would boost my earnings to eighteen thousand dollars. No sooner had I sat down in Paul's office than he said: "Well, let's see, we paid you a twelve-thousand-dollar salary last year, so of course we work from there." After a moment of shock, I said, "No." And then I said, "No, no, no. That's not the way I look at it. Salary, bonus—they're all the same to me. I made fifteen thousand dollars last year. I have to talk up from fifteen."

We hassled for a while and finally I agreed to sign for seventeen thousand dollars. I thought, "I had a pretty good year but I guess one year doesn't really prove much." Still, I was unhappy at taking one thousand dollars less than I'd asked for, and I think Paul understood right then that it was not my way to set an asking price with the idea of coming down and compromising. I haven't much stomach for haggling, and I have a lot of regard for the truth. So I ask the price I'm convinced I deserve.

Now that I'd had a taste of bargaining following my rookie year, I realized that it was unlikely that I would get the money I wanted just by going in and asking for it. I wasn't quite sure what else I could do, but a boisterous outlander named Frank Lane came along at just the right time and furnished an answer.

In 1958—my second season—I set an all-time N.F.L. rushing record of 1527 yards and tied the league's touchdown record, scoring eighteen in one season. Sportswriters raved about me. Photographers cornered me in front of my locker and photographed me stripped to the waist, biceps flexed and muscles bulging. Splashed across the newspapers and magazines were histories of my athletic career that detailed my exploits on the football field, on the basketball court, on the cinder track, and even on the lacrosse field. I was pictured as a man of almost limitless athletic talents. When the season came to a close I settled back for the winter to ponder how much money I was worth to the Browns.

Meanwhile, over at Cleveland Stadium, which quartered the offices of both the Browns and the Cleveland Indians baseball club, Indian general manager Frank Lane was pondering ways of drumming up a little midwinter excitement over his club. He hit upon an idea that was scarcely calculated to improve the disposition of his football counterpart down the hall.

Lane sent a letter to me inviting me to report to the Indians' spring training camp in Tucson. He did not specify the position he had in mind for me, but he expressed the strong belief that a man of my athletic versatility could make the grade in big-league baseball. He stated that if I indicated possibilities he would be willing to go top dollar to sign me. He also had the presence of mind to invite the sportswriters to lunch and pass the word along. They had little enough to write about at that time of year, and Frank Lane was one of America's great creative minds when it came to seizing an opportunity for publicity.

"We're not after cheap publicity," he intoned. "If he comes to camp and has what it takes, we'll go from there on money. Even Bill Skiff of the Yankees has mentioned that Jim was a great prospect," Lane went on, citing expert scouting testimony.

Naturally my telephone rang. The press wanted my reaction.

"I haven't talked to Mr. Lane yet," I said, striving to be coy. "However, his proposal surely bears looking into."

I hadn't played a game of baseball in years and certainly had no notion that I could go out and make the big leagues. Still, there were reasons why nobody could entirely dismiss the possibility that Lane and I might be serious.

"In high school and sandlot leagues on Long Island," I read of myself in the newspaper, "he impressed scouts with his talent."

Well, it was true that the Yankees and Braves had offered to sign me. Casey Stengel had written me. Honey Russell, a Braves scout, had tailed me. But my guess is that they were interested in me only because of my size and speed. In my senior year of high school, I pitched a few good games but no no-hitters, and I played first base and hit about .285, which is no sensational high school average. Actually, baseball was my weakest sport. But I wasn't about to call this to the attention of the press.

Frank Lane's proposal, viewed from a purely mercenary perspective, was pregnant with the possibility that he could indeed give me a whopping salary and get his investment back quickly. He could nurse me along as a pitcher in spring training, shouting as only he could about the great improvement I was showing each week, and then wheel me into vast Cleveland Stadium for a debut that would pack the house with the curious. Presto, he would have his money back and then some. And who knows? As the season wore on, I might even show signs of becoming a baseball player.

I'm not saying Frank Lane had any such scheme in mind, but it was something to think about. I wouldn't be surprised if Paul Brown and Lane weren't on speaking terms for a while after Lane sent me that letter. In any case, I soon went to Paul's office to talk contract.

I'd decided to hit Paul for an eight-thousand-dollar raise that would hike my salary to twenty-five thousand dollars. I said to myself, "Last year I accepted a two-thousand-dollar raise after I'd led the league in rushing. Looking back now, I think a five-thousand-dollar raise would have been in order. I think a five-thousand dollar raise is in order now, but I'm going to make up for the money I lost last year by asking eight thousand dollars."

I stated my price to Paul and he said, "I don't think we can go that high. You're making seventeen thousand dollars now and that puts you right up there with Groza as the highest paid on the club. You're asking twenty-five thousand dollars and that's a lot of money. I'd be willing to go to twenty-two thousand dollars."

I stuck to my guns. Paul pursed his lips and looked upset. But I kept saying twenty-five thousand dollars and sat there stroking my pitching arm. Finally, he agreed to my price and bade me goodbye in good humor. I hadn't even had to bring up Frank Lane's name. I have no idea whether Lane's stunt worried Paul, but it certainly hadn't done me any harm.

As a twenty-five-thousand-dollar fullback in 1959, my rushing yardage dropped off from 1527 to 1329, but that figure was still better than any ball carrier had registered in the history of the league. So I wanted another substantial raise. I expected a battle from Paul. But once again, I received outside assistance.

During the off-season a young Cleveland boxer named Ernie Burford, who was a friend of mine, came to me and asked me to help him straighten out his affairs. Ernie was managed by Al Naiman, a businessman who dabbled in boxing. Ernie felt that he could go farther under a manager more prominent in boxing circles. We went to see Naiman and he graciously released Ernie from their contract. Ernie then said to me, "Do you think you can help me find a good manager?"

I put in a call to Norm Rothschild, the well-known Syracuse promoter with whom I'd become friendly during my college days. As a matter of fact, Norm frequently had urged me to turn to boxing, saying he was convinced I could become heavyweight champion, but I'd never taken his advice seriously. Anyhow, I telephoned him now and asked him to recommend a manager for

Ernie, and he suggested Marv Jensen, the Utah mink rancher who managed middleweight champion Gene Fullmer.

When I phoned Jensen he said, "Get on a plane with the boy and fly out here to Ogden and we'll talk about it." We flew to Ogden and Jensen signed Ernie to a contract and then informed me that he wanted me to sign a contract, too. "Norm Rothschild and I will guarantee you $150,000 your first year. We're dead serious. We'll put the money in escrow to prove it."

I had no urge to be a boxer, simply because I didn't like the idea of having cauliflower ears. Still, $150,000 was no figure to sniff at, and I was truly interested. I told Jensen I'd never boxed and had no idea whether I had the ability to be a fighter, or even the chin to be one, but he said, "Tell you what–come out here for two weeks and work out. If you like boxing after two weeks, we'll draw up the papers. I think you'll like fighting. You can be heavyweight champion within three years."

By a neat coincidence, the Jensen-Rothschild offer had come along in advance of my 1960 contract negotiations with Paul. Not only did the offer interest me but it occurred to me that even if I decided I wanted no part of boxing my bargaining position with the Browns had improved. I casually told a newspaperman of the boxing offer, and it hit the headlines.

Determined to stay on the attack, I stated during a banquet stopover in Charleston, West Virginia: "I haven't signed for next season and unless it's for what I think it ought to be, I'll quit. The coaches in professional football seem to think there's a limit on salaries."

"His contract," retorted Paul, "was so high last season that I may have gone overboard. . . . In any case, we don't do business this way."

I liked doing business this way. Oldtime boxers charged into print with advice for me. A little fuel never hurt a fire.

Paul's tack, meanwhile, was "Jim always has a good story

ready at this time of year." The fact was, I had not only one good story but two.

Of late, I'd been holding down a job in the Pepsi-Cola marketing division. Pepsi-Cola had not hired me merely for the sake of a little publicity, nor was my job only part-time. I was on salary and on call year 'round. The job paid me ten thousand dollars. I had taken it with the understanding that I was building a place for myself in the company and would continue to work for Pepsi long after I'd retired from football. I could retire any time I chose and report straight to Pepsi's New York office.

Certainly if I left football I'd suffer a loss in income, but I'd get a salary of thirteen or fourteen thousand dollars and have a secure future ahead of me. My prospects were bright. Harvey Russell, my immediate boss, was moving up fast in the corporation. He was soon to be promoted to Vice-President for Special Markets—that is, ethnic and national groups. In addition to the Negro market, Pepsi had developed rather heavy markets in Mexico and among the Spanish-speaking peoples of the U.S. I began to seriously consider early retirement, knowing that football is no lifetime job and that moreover, an injury can cut a man's career short before he's even reached his peak.

In the last analysis, I decided that I would stay in football if Paul Brown met my salary demands; if he did not, I had the Pepsi-Cola Company and the Jensen-Rothschild money as alternatives. Paul Brown had to think about that, because these were offers I hadn't fabricated.

My campaign for a raise was moving along nicely in the newspapers. FORGET RING CAREER, DEMPSEY TELLS J. BROWN, sang a headline. I appreciated Jack Dempsey's concern for my safety and the ink he contributed to my salary campaign. I was beginning to feel at home in the slick realm of public relations, and like a good PR man I was determined to be ready for any counter-tactics Paul might have in mind.

Paul, I knew, was no dummy when it came to putting out

publicity releases. The classic case, if I may jump ahead for the moment to the year 1962, was a release in which he struck back at Milt Plum. Milt, after having led the league in passing in 1961, had tailed off in '62 and blamed Paul's rigid messenger system for having put him in a tactically impossible position. Desperate to call his own plays, Milt had taken the drastic step of giving a newspaper interview in which he drew the issue in no uncertain terms. Paul responded by trading him to Detroit, but even then, Paul was not finished with Milt. Milt had talked back. Now Milt would get his.

The front office released a statistical study showing that in his most recent season 70 percent of Milt's passes had traveled only seven yards or less, and that approximately one out of three never got beyond the line of scrimmage. A damning publicity release if there ever was one.

All of us on the team knew that (a) Paul called the pass plays, and (b) one of our frequent plays was a short flare pass behind the line of scrimmage. Milt fired back at the front-office release, but somehow, rebuttals usually have the sound of whining.

In 1960, as I prepared to go into Paul's office to talk contract, I vowed, "If I come out of there without a contract, I'm at least not going to get caught in a position where I have to whine." I rang up the sports department of the *Plain Dealer,* Cleveland's morning paper, and asked for Chuck Heaton, the *Plain Dealer* football writer.

"Chuck, I'm going in to talk contract with Paul today," I said. "I may have a statement for you as soon as I get out of there, so I'd appreciate it if you'll stand by for a call."

If Paul and I were unable to agree on salary, I was going to make the *Plain Dealer's* first edition with my side of the story. I had no intention of letting the club get into print first, forcing me to make a rebuttal. I walked into Paul's office feeling real Madison Avenue. My preparations turned out to be unnecessary.

"How does thirty thousand dollars sound to you?" Paul said to me. "That's a nice five-thousand-dollar raise."

"I had thirty-two thousand dollars in mind," I replied. "I don't think that's too high."

"Tell you what," said Paul. "I'll go to thirty-two if you sign for two years."

Why a two-year contract? The answer was that the league already had laid plans to expand its twelve-game schedule to fourteen games the following year—1961. Logically, players would want more money for playing more games. Paul wanted a two-year contract under his belt so he wouldn't have to bargain with me the next year when I'd have an additional point in my favor.

Rumors of an expanded schedule already had been circulating among N.F.L. players, for a number of them had been asked to sign two-year contracts. We knew something was up. I thought about Paul's offer and said to myself, "Well, seven thousand's a good raise and how much higher than thirty-two thousand dollars can I go anyway?" Baltimore quarterback Johnny Unitas reportedly was the league's highest-paid player at thirty-one thousand dollars. So I signed for two years and walked out of Paul's office probably the highest paid man in football. I never dreamed at the time that eventually I would go a lot higher than thirty-two thousand dollars and do it without a peep of opposition from Paul.

In 1962, I met Paul across the bargaining table for the last time. My thirty-two-thousand-dollar, two-year contract had expired, but in the interim much had happened to broaden my horizons. When the fourteen-game schedule went into effect in 1961, pro football burst into an era of unprecedented profits. The public appetite had proved more than willing to consume fourteen games. Moreover, I suddenly found myself in the unique position of being on the inside of the front office looking out. Four years earlier I had helped recruit Ernie Davis for Syracuse, and now, by the strange designs of fate, I was called upon to take part in negotiations between Ernie and the Browns.

The previous year Art Modell and R. J. (Rudy) Schaefer, the Schaefer beer tycoon, had bought control of the Browns and immediately had issued a public statement of absolute confidence in Paul. They even gave him a new eight-year contract, which in time was to make him the nation's highest-paid golfer. Paul soon exercised his continued authority by transacting a player deal that painted club president Modell into an uncomfortable corner. Washington had drafted Ernie Davis but hadn't signed him yet. Paul wanted Ernie, and so without bothering to consult Art he traded Bobby Mitchell and a first draft choice to the Redskins in exchange for rights to Ernie.

Now, if the Browns let Ernie get away to the American Football League, Art Modell would look like a cheapskate; and worse, the Browns would be minus the great Bobby Mitchell and have nothing to show for the trade. So Art was going to have to dig deep into the treasury whether he liked it or not.

My role in the negotiations was a curious one, because I represented both sides.

In preparation for turning pro, Ernie had taken the identical step that I had in my senior year at Syracuse. He placed the negotiations in the hands of a trusted hometown attorney–Tony DeFilippo of Elmira, N.Y. DeFilippo made an intensive investigation of pro football's financial structure in an effort to determine a fair asking price for Ernie, and in the course of his investigation he called upon me for my views. I had no qualms about helping Ernie prepare to argue money with the Browns, for Art Modell was aware of my participation and had no objection to it. As a friend of both Ernie and Art, I was in a position to honestly advocate that on the one hand, Ernie demand stiff terms, and on the other hand, that he lean toward the N.F.L., the toughest league, as a matter of personal pride and confidence in his own ability to succeed. Notwithstanding my personal coolness to Paul Brown, I was able to assure Ernie with all honesty that Paul would provide a good showcase for his talents. I knew that Paul planned to adopt the so-called big back system that Vince Lombardi had popularized with Jim Taylor and Paul Hornung at Green Bay. Ernie and I would be teamed up.

Actually, when Modell sat down in Elmira with Ernie and Tony DeFilippo to make his final pitch, my presence was welcomed by both sides. I took this as an expression of confidence in my forthrightness, and was touched by it and deeply grateful.

In the end, Ernie signed with Art Modell for less money than he was offered by Buffalo of the American Football League. Still, he received a whopping deal—a fifteen-thousand-dollar bonus, a three-year contract calling for a total of sixty-five thousand dollars in salary, an off-season job, and a judicious arrangement by which his money would be conservatively invested while he received only enough cash to live in modest comfort.

Naturally, inasmuch as I knew the Browns were paying tremendous money for Ernie, it did not appear unseemly that I take a somewhat expanded view of my own earning potential.

Cleveland newspapers were speculating that I would ask fifty thousand dollars. I really hadn't thought of asking that much, but Tony DeFilippo said to me, "Ask for sixty thousand."

I said, "Sonofagun, that's a lot of money." I took Tony's advice and asked for sixty, but my heart wasn't in it. I felt I was asking too much. It was the first time I'd stated a figure to Paul Brown without being certain in my heart that I deserved it. Consequently, he had no difficulty getting me to come down.

I signed for forty-five thousand dollars with the stipulation that if we won the Eastern Conference title I would get a five-thousand-dollar bonus. And if that happened, I would pick up perhaps five thousand dollars more in proceeds from the championship game purse. So if all went well, I'd make approximately fifty-five thousand dollars. To lighten my tax load I arranged to draw only a portion of my salary, leaving the balance in the hands of the ball club with the understanding that I could claim it within a five-year period following my retirement.

My 1962 contract made me far and away the highest paid player in the game, and I was struck by a singular aspect of my negotiations with Paul. He was downright sweet throughout. The thought crossed my mind that since Art Modell and Rudy Schaefer had bought Paul's stock in the club, Paul no longer was parting with his own money at contract time.

Ever since Paul left following the 1962 season, I've negotiated my contracts directly with Art. "Negotiate" isn't really the right word, however. I haven't had to negotiate with him. There is no fairer employer in pro football.

In 1962 I had what most people consider my worst season. I gained a lot of yards—996 to be exact—but it was the first time since my rookie year that I'd failed to reach the one thousand-yard mark and the first time in my career that I failed to lead the league in rushing. Jim Taylor won that title. Through most of the season I'd played with a badly sprained right wrist that made it difficult for me to handle the ball and distracted me in open field where I like to shift the ball from hand to hand, but I did not have to call Art's attention to my injury. He knew his people. Indeed, he raised my pay.

To how much? I'm not saying. I work for the man, so I'll abide by pro football's unwritten law that salaries remain secret. Art probably wouldn't mind my revealing my pay were it not for the fact that when he truthfully told the press he was paying eighty thousand dollars for Ernie Davis, the other clubowners jumped on his back. I can't put them on Art's back again. He's my man. If I ever let him down I'll never be able to face myself in the mirror.

No longer need I look for a Frank Lane or a Marv Jensen or a Pepsi-Cola Company to buttress my bargaining position. Art Modell went around telling people, "You know what we call our fullback? We call him Big Jim." He wasn't talking about my size. He meant that he had a regard for me, that he felt I had the character to provide a positive example for the team.

In other words, I no longer was Paul Brown's big brute.

PART II

THE SCUPPERNONG HULL

CHAPTER 1

My roots

"Be home by sundown or I'll take a switch to you, Nathaniel. You hear?"

I was Nathaniel–James Nathaniel Brown. She was a little wisp of a woman–how old I have no idea. But old, that's for sure. She was my great-grandmother. Her name was Nora Petersen, but to me she was mama. She was all I had, and I was all she had.

Sometimes I'd stay out late and then sneak through the back door. I'd tiptoe to my room, get in bed, and fall asleep. Suddenly I'd be awakened by the sting of a birch switch on my backside. Little old mama would stand there and whale the daylights out of me.

I knew I had a real mother but she lived up North in a place called New York. She'd gone there for work when I was two. "Someday she'll send for you," mama would tell me. Meanwhile, mama was going to see that I was raised proper. I scrubbed behind my ears and went to the Baptist church every Sunday morning and once in a while wondered what my mother would be like, and whether New York boys were good at carving slingshots and climbing plum trees.

At the time, I didn't know my father at all. He and my mother had separated shortly after I was born. I was their only child and all they had left behind on St. Simons Island, a sleepy, semi-tropical fragment of Georgia lying in the Atlantic Ocean just off the mainland. My mother was Theresa Brown, hard-working domestic. My father was Swinton (Sweet Sue) Brown, gambling man.

People told me that Sue—his friends called him just plain Sue—was a huge man who had been a good football player in nearby Brunswick, Georgia, and had boxed professionally around the state. They also said he loved to dance and fancied himself a man about town. Everyone who told me about Sue spoke of him with affection, because he was, by all accounts, impossible to dislike. It just happened that he had a weakness for the dice and cards. Sue always figured that Lady Luck was due to smile on him, but she mostly turned her back. This was why his marriage broke up. My mother loved him but she just couldn't run a household on inside straights that didn't fill.

So she went north to start fresh. And Sue, too, migrated to New York, as so many southern Negroes were doing. Left behind, I spent the first eight years of my life on St. Simons Island. My family consisted of mama and Aunt Bertha Powell and Grandmother Myrtle Powell, who lived together in mama's one-story house. Contrary to romantic accounts that have been published, I did not grow up in a cabin. Mama's house was a spacious dwelling of white frame, though a little weatherbeaten and growing brownish.

Had I never returned to St. Simons Island when I was old enough to know I was a second-class citizen there, I'd have nothing but fond memories of the place. St. Simons is one of a string of islands scattered along almost 150 miles of Georgia coastline and known as "Georgia's Golden Isles." As a small boy I could throw a stone from the beach and hit Sea Island, the famous resort where millionaires go to golf and sunbathe. Our own beaches were pure white sand, as beautiful as any natural beaches I've ever seen. Rimming the south tip of our island were shops and summer homes owned by well-to-do white folks from the mainland. Thirteen miles long and as much as seven miles wide at one point, St. Simons was much bigger than Sea Island but had no more than a few hundred permanent inhabitants when I was a little guy. My island was an undiscovered thing of beauty. There were palm trees, fig trees, grapefruit trees, orange trees, pecan trees, and even a few banana trees–all worthy of climbing. There were moss-hung oak and cypress and cedar and longleaf pine and magnolia. I could reach out and pluck a handful of delicious scuppernong grapes–green grapes that grew brown and sweet when they ripened. I could sit by the ocean and watch the porpoise roll in the surf and count the sandcrabs scurrying across the beach. Or I could run down the dirt roads into the dark woods and murky marshland and come upon crystal clear ponds for swimming and diving. In the ponds were alligator bones that enabled us kids to perpetuate–for our own excitement–the tales of alligators still roaming the island.

We even dug for treasure that was supposed to have been buried by pirates back in the woods. "Don't talk, 'cause if you talk while you're diggin', the treasure sinks deeper."

We played in the ruins of Oglethorpe's fort, where the British had defeated the Spanish in the Battle of Bloody Marsh. It seems strange that it was on obscure St. Simons Island that Spain lost its grip on southeastern America; and strange, too, there had once been fine cotton plantations on our sleepy island. But after the Civil War, St. Simons had gone to sleep. I was past my sixth birthday when the Navy put a World War II air base on St. Simons and caused the island to stir with new population.

There were, of course, no Little Leagues or Midget Leagues on our island–no adults who felt it their duty to furnish us with bats and balls and uniforms and to schedule our time and give us complexes. Consequently, we learned to do for ourselves. We had no basketball court or football field or baseball field, but we'd find a length of board and a rubber ball and play a stickball-type game. We made a real skill of rolling tires with sticks at top speed.

We carved slingshots and bows and arrows and once even fashioned a rowboat that stayed afloat in the pond for fifteen minutes.

I wonder if the Little Leagues and Midget Leagues allow today's kids time to go crabbing. I loved to sit on the edge of the pier and drop my crab basket to the floor of the ocean. My crab basket was a square cage made of wire net. It had four gates, each with a string tied to it. The four strings were tied to a longer string that I held on the pier. I would put a piece of meat in the middle of the basket, then drop the basket down and by relaxing the control string open the four gates. I couldn't see down to the bottom of the ocean, so I would sit there and try to guess whether Mr. Crab had come for supper. If I guessed right, I'd pull the string taut and close the gates at the very time he was inside feasting.

At the end of the day I'd have a bushelbasket of crabs and would boil them in water and pick out the meat. Over on Sea Island the millionaires were paying fancy prices for the same crabmeat.

I suppose that in a sense I was born to be a fullback, because even as a little guy I was rough and tough. Mama called me Nathaniel and others called me Nate, but many of the kids called me Man. I was the hull of the scuppernong grape—tougher than the hull of any other grape. The kids on St. Simons thought I was a little crazy because I'd fight anybody, no matter how much older and bigger than I. It wasn't that I was belligerent—I just liked rough contact.

We were poor down on St. Simons but not poor enough to matter. Most of the Negroes lived back on dirt roads in the island's interior, where they raised a few pigs or a few horses or chickens. But mama's house stood only two miles from the beach on a paved road that led straight down to the village and beach. We lived in the first group of Negroes—the more reputable Negro section, one might say. We had four bedrooms, a living room, a dining room, a kitchen, and a screened-in porch in the rear where

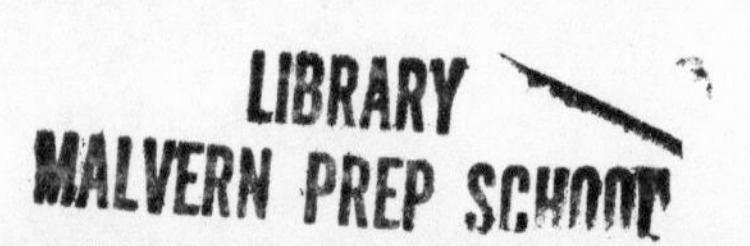

we usually ate. We had fig trees and pecan trees in the yard. I wasn't old enough to know exactly how we got enough money to keep us going, but I know that Aunt Bertha worked and I had an uncle who owned a cab in New York and sent us money. One way or another, we got by.

I was happy. I didn't spend much time thinking about the fact that I didn't have a mother and father. I played with white kids and Negro kids alike and enjoyed my reputation as a tough little guy. I played on the white man's beaches without being chased, because I was what is patronizingly referred to as "a cute little pickaninny." I suppose I amused the vacationers.

Mama sent me off to school one day—to a two-room Negro schoolhouse that lay deep inland and had one teacher to handle all elementary grades. Even then, it didn't occur to me that I was a second-class American. Segregated schooling seemed the natural order of things. Mama had never taught me to resent.

Luckily, my mother sent for me before I was old enough to realize my status and grow bitter on St. Simons. She'd saved a few dollars and had found a "sleep-in" job doing housework for a family who provided her with a small apartment. So mama packed me a big lunch and put me on the train for New York.

I loved mama deeply but I wasn't heartbroken to leave her, simply because she'd done a good job of preparing me for the day. She'd always reminded me that some day I'd go North to join my mother, and had built up the reunion as a joyous occasion. So I had come to accept it as inevitable, and even to welcome it. Then, too, I was promised that I'd be able to come home to St. Simons for summer vacations, and I did for many years. St. Simons was my island in the sun, and I was almost like the rich folks who came only for the summer. I'd come home like a big shot and brag to the other kids about life in New York, as if I lived a life of adventure in the big city. With a certain air of snobbery I would tell them that folks in New York pronounced the word "the" thuh—not "thee," as it was pronounced on St. Simons.

But coming home was not all fun. Now I was old enough to be told to do my swimming at an obscure beach on the hind side of the island. I hadn't even known there was such a thing as a nigger beach. Now, too, I learned that white kids threw rocks at you, and you'd better be prepared to throw rocks back.

I recall walking down to the docks one day and seeing a white boy fishing off the pier. I stopped to talk with him. He had an extra rod and an extra reel and offered them to me. We fished there for a while, and then we went surf fishing. It was a good day, and I suppose it has stuck in my mind because it showed that boys are born good and might remain that way if adults didn't get around to hammering bigotry into them.

The last time I visited St. Simons Island I had an experience that made me know I'd probably never return. I'd become, by then, a nationally known college football star. Mama was dead but I wanted to go home and visit Aunt Bertha and Grandmother Myrtle. When I got there Myrtle told me she was doing housework for a white family and that when she had mentioned to them that I was coming home the man of the house said to her: "Ask the boy to come over and visit a spell. I'd like to meet him."

I drove out to his house and knocked on the door. Myrtle's employer answered the door and stepped outside and shook my hand. "Well," he said, "I'm certainly glad to meet you, son. I've followed your career at Syracuse, and we're sure proud of you down here." He stood there in front of the door for quite a while, telling me how I'd done myself proud and telling me what a good worker Myrtle was. He had nothing but kind words. But I said to myself: "This is a lot of crap. He asks me to drive out here so he can shake my hand and tell me what a big man I am, but he doesn't invite me inside and offer me a seat. He's glad to meet me, but I'm not worthy of common courtesy."

I was more saddened than angry. I said goodbye to my island in the sun, the wonderful place where I'd hung my crab basket from the pier and hunted buried treasure in the woods. I've never gone back.

CHAPTER 2

I was a teen-age warlord

(BUT PLEASE, FELLAS, NO KNIVES)

Psychologists, sociologists, and writers are fond of blaming juvenile delinquency and a variety of other disturbances on broken homes. I am not learned in such matters except for the fact that unlike many of the psychologists, sociologists, and writers, I happen to have come from a broken home. It's my opinion that the experts have given us poor children of misfortune a little too much sympathy.

As a child, I liked movies. I was always a self-reliant kid, and consequently thought nothing of going to a movie alone. The upshot of this was that years later a national magazine writer searched into my past and came up with the verdict that I had been driven by pangs of insecurity to retreat into the darkness of theaters. Actually I just liked Cary Grant, Gary Cooper, and many of the other actors.

I get a little weary of hearing broken homes blamed for 96.3 percent of American youth's difficulties. John Wooten, a big Cleveland lineman who opens up holes for me to run through, comes from a broken home, and he and I have discussed the effect that such an environment has on children. We search our memories to recall when and how we suffered torment, but we find little to go on.

My guess is that thanks to all the yakking about broken homes, a lot of kids have found a good excuse to get into trouble. The broken home is their crutch in Juvenile Court. I am not dogmatic about this. Looking back on my own boyhood, there were many times when I came perilously close to becoming a no-account. It took a kind word here and a guiding hand there to point me in the right direction. My teachers appealed to my better judgment. And so I submit that almost every kid at one time or another is given an opportunity to respond to similar kindnesses, but he is less likely to respond when he has learned in advance that he possesses a ready-made excuse—the broken home—for irresponsibility.

By rough count, my mother and Sweet Sue reconciled four times during my youth but never for long. Sue worked at a variety of jobs—porter, caddy, waiter, etc.—but found himself unable to embrace the concept of permanent employment. He would earn a few dollars, then turn his attention to the gaming tables.

I never came to know him well, or at least not nearly as well as other kids knew their fathers, but I liked Sue very much. Whenever he was around we were always running footraces. Not once did I beat him. He had a good heart and was what you might call a responsible gambler. He gambled with his own money, never with my mother's. And each time he left us, another reconciliation over, he would tell me: "Treat your mother good. You may not always like what she tells you to do, but understand she's telling you for your own good." Sue passed in and out of my life as if his coming and going were no more than the design by which we were to live. I did not miss having a father.

When I first arrived in the North at the age of nine, my mother was employed by a Jewish family—the Brockmans—who lived in the well-to-do, all-white suburb of Great Neck, Long Island. They provided us with a small one-bedroom apartment off the kitchen. However, I had to attend school several miles away in Manhasset, a community that ranged from comfortably middle class to very poor. The poor lived in an area called "the Valley," which was ripe with slums that made the community fathers wince. Visible to motorists passing down Northern Boulevard through Manhasset, the slums were regarded as a bad advertisement for the town and later were torn down and replaced by a park and a housing project.

In Manhasset, Nate Brown became Jimmy Brown. At school I enrolled as James Nathaniel Brown, so the teachers called me James and the kids made it Jimmy. Many of the kids in my elementary school were from the poor Valley district, and I found out my first day in school that the student body was tough. I wasted no time fighting my way to the top.

That first day, my mother dressed me neat-as-a-pin in a starched shirt and creased trousers; she brushed my hair and sent me off to school in a taxi. The student body took note of my arrival. At recess in the schoolyard, a Negro boy–no bigger nor smaller than I–addressed me. "You look real pretty, Sis," he said, and promptly shoved me back on my heels. "Well, good," I thought. Manhasset was going to be just as playful as St. Simons Island. I knocked him down and dove on top of him and began punching the daylights out of him. "Dirty fighter!" all the kids hollered. I stopped punching and looked up, mystified. Down on the island, this was the way we always fought. The purpose of knocking someone down was to sit on him and get in the best licks. Nobody back home called it dirty fighting.

Anyhow, while I was trying to decide whether to go on, a man whom the kids called Bulldog Drummond strode into the schoolyard and yanked me off my new friend. Bulldog Drummond was the school principal, Mr. Hutchens. The kids had named him after the hero of the radio program because Mr. Hutchens had a square jaw and was old-fashioned tough.

"I'll show you how we settle these things here," Mr. Hutchens told me. He marched us into the gym and handed us boxing gloves. I'd never seen a pair of boxing gloves. My opponent, having been marched to the gym by Mr. Hutchens on previous occasions, knew how to use the gloves. He gave me a licking. "These northerners have a funny way of doing things," I thought, but out of sight of Mr. Hutchens I managed to win all my fights and become known as a tough guy. My mother continued to send me off to school in a taxi, all starched and spotless.

The Brockmans were wonderful people to live with. They bought me my first basketball and hung a basket for me in the yard. They did more things for me than I can remember, and even after they moved to Los Angeles several years later, they continued to correspond with my mother and send her gifts. I would have liked to have lived with the Brockmans all my boyhood, but after perhaps two years there I was too old to live with my mother in a one-bedroom apartment. The Brockmans, with children of their own, had given us all the space they could, so my mother roomed me out with a Negro family in Manhasset.

I wasn't happy in Manhasset. The lady of the house was very religious. She was, no doubt, a good woman but quite stern. Somehow, I felt like an intruder.

Happily, I always saw my mother on weekends. I loved my mother as much as any son would, and yet I was never able to bring myself to call her mama. Mama was my great-grandmother, down on St. Simons. I didn't know what to call my mother. Once in a while I called her mother, but the word always sounded strange on my lips. I had known affection from my great-grandmother and had returned it, but was never able to demonstrate, overtly, my affection for my mother. This hurt her, I know. But in a way, I had two mothers, and mama had gotten there first.

When the Brockmans moved to Los Angeles, my mother took a first-floor flat in Manhasset and brought me to live with her again, and I was happy once more. Her expenses were higher and she had trouble finding enough work, but with a lot of scraping she managed to keep me neatly dressed. My neatness had become a point of pride with me, and later, my high school football coach, Ed Walsh, came to realize this. "How'd you like to take a trip into Manhattan with me tomorrow?" he said to me one day. The next day I found myself standing in a Howard's store, where Ed Walsh had me fitted for a fine suit.

My coaches and teachers were the big people in my life. The Lord knows, they had their work cut out for them in trying to make something of me, but they went at it.

I had no interest in studies and, what's more, had become president and official warlord of a teen-age gang known as the Gaylords. We held dances and parties and with the ticket receipts decked ourselves out in reversible jackets–base black with orchid trim on one side and base orchid with black trim on the other. We had our gang name lettered across our backs and our own names in front. The jackets were a big deal.

Many teen-age gangs roamed a string of communities across Long Island, picking up girls and attending rival gangs' parties uninvited. Our Long Island gangs, however, were not of the zip gun variety known to Brooklyn. Our boys carried switchblade penknives but only to build up their own egos. They liked to stand on street corners clicking their knives, but they never used them in fights. Fights generally wound up with an enactment of the *West Side Story* bit–that is, warlord pitted against warlord, with everyone else forming a circle.

As warlord of the Gaylords, I rarely had to fight, simply because my opponents almost always backed down. Since my first year on Long Island–the year I'd fought my way to the top of the class–I'd had a fairly formidable reputation. Still, I should have known that sooner or later I'd have to face a blade. One night in Hempstead I did.

We had invited ourselves to a party being held by a rival gang. For a while, all was peaceful. I was just standing there, listening to the phonograph music and minding my own business. The rival warlord, however, had been drinking liquor and growing belligerent on it. He swayed with the music and snapped his fingers and then, pretending to be only releasing his feeling for the music, gave me a hard slap on the back. I knew he meant it as a challenge. I said nothing. He slapped me a second time, and I told him, "Look, don't slap me on the back." I moved a few steps away. "Oh, you think you're something big?" he said. "You guys come in here in your sharp jackets and think you're something." I said to myself, "Here it goes." I told him, "Look, we can settle this fast. Just come outside." He got loud. "Sure I'll come outside," he shouted for everyone to hear. "I'll wipe up the street with you." We went outside, and everyone crowded around us. Then, click! Out came his blade.

I had no knife myself. I never carried one, because I never believed a knife would make me any bigger and I knew I could never cut anyone. Now I had to think fast. I reached into my pocket and held my hand there for a menacing moment. All I had in it was a ringful of keys. With a great show of purpose, I worked one key into position so that it pointed sharply against my trousers. Then I whipped my hand from my pocket. The instant I did, my opponent closed his knife and shoved it into his pocket. He smiled weakly. I opened the palm of my hand, revealing a fistful of keys, and then hauled off with my other hand —also open—and gave him a hard slap in the face. End of *West Side Story* bit. "Let's go home," I said to the Gaylords.

Actually, I guess I never quite fit the image of a gang warlord. Though I never minded a fight, I never picked one and I disliked bullies. Kids sometimes teased me for not smoking or drinking liquor, but I couldn't see how a cigaret dangling from the corner of my mouth could make me any tougher. Then, too, I was coming to realize that my physical strength could be put to better use on a ball field than in fist fights.

A succession of great men—men who were great simply because they cared—had come into my life:

First, there was Jay Stranahan, coach of the basketball, lacrosse, and six-man football teams at Plandome Road Junior

High. "Jimmy, you have tremendous athletic ability," he told me. "Don't waste it." There had been no such thing as football on St. Simons Island; the first game I'd seen in Manhasset had been on a corner lot that had been picked clean of rocks and broken glass. Now Jay Stranahan was telling me that I could play this game—and lacrosse and basketball, too—better than any kid in school, and he meant to give me no time to get into trouble.

Then there was Jack Peploe, a cop. Patrolman Jack Peploe, today superintendent of parks and grounds for Nassau County, ran the Police Boys Club. He put me in charge of the Boys Club basketball team. He gave me the keys to the high school gym and appointed me the big shot to open the gym every night.

There were others—people all around me who without hesitation went out of their way to make something of me. Mrs. Virginia Hansen, a speech teacher, observed that I was a quiet kid. She forced me to make two- and three-minute speeches in school and brought me to the point where I became a self-assured assembly speaker. Al Dawson, the high school track coach, worked tirelessly to develop my skills. Dr. Raymond L. Collins, superintendent of Manhasset schools, took me to the school gym Sunday afternoons to shoot baskets with him and his son. (Dr. Collins was an old-fashioned underhand set shooter but probably the deadliest shot of all school superintendents in the country.) In short, what I received from these adults around me was love. I was a poor kid from a broken home but I was not insecure, because where there is love there cannot be insecurity. Even when I was a little guy on St. Simons Island, mama and I never felt insecure because we loved one another and knew that come what may, we were not alone.

At Manhasset High School there was a football coach named Ed Walsh, and I will tell you about him because he was my idea of a saint. He was a slender, soft-spoken man but one whose actions made you realize that real strength was not physical strength but strength of character. I am convinced that Ed Walsh had not one iota of bigotry in him. Moreover, of all the football coaches I've played for, Ed, a mere high school coach, was the finest—the most expert. Even today, when I find it necessary to refresh my knowledge of fundamentals, I say to myself, "Let's see, how did Ed Walsh teach that move?" In the four years I played for him, his teams lost only two games—one by a touchdown and the other by a single point. Because he had movies made of his games, I've been able to go back to Manhasset from time to time and watch myself in action as a high school halfback. It's hard to believe, but I made better moves and cuts in high school than I've made in college and pro ball, and that's a fact.

More than a great teacher of football technique, Ed Walsh was a builder of character. He cared about his kids, and would reach into his own pocket to buy a needy student clothing. I had a childish spat with my mother once and told Ed I was going to leave home. "Come out and stay at my house a while," he told me, "until you've had a chance to think it over and you're sure you're doing the right thing." It was no phony gesture but a sincere invitation.

"You can be a professional football player," he told me on another occasion. "But you've got to go to college first, and you won't go to college unless you start taking your studies seriously." I began taking my studies seriously. In time I was nominated for student body president but said I wouldn't run, because I knew that if I were elected it would be only because of my popularity as an athlete. I felt one of the topmost students should be president. So I was elected chief justice of the student court, which though a lesser post was a step up from gang warlord.

"Okay, Jimmy," Ed Walsh barked at me one day in football scrimmage. "If you want to loaf get off the first team. Get over there on defense with the second team." I went over to the defense and did all I could to tear the first team apart. The next day I was back on the first team. The point is, I had to get back into Ed Walsh's good graces at all costs, not so much because I disliked being second-string but because I had let him down. Since that day I've never messed up on a coach of his stripe—that is, a coach I could talk to and reason with and who would give me the benefit of the doubt in a tough spot.

Not long after I started playing for Ed Walsh, still another adult came into my life. Viewed in the stereotype, he was that great buffoon of the American scene—the sports-minded college alumnus who is out to recruit star athletes for the alma mater. One night he came out to see our team play. Specifically, he wanted to look over a quarterback named Bobby Brink.

He thought Bobby Brink was a little slow for topflight football (though Bobby later played for Yale), but I caught his eye and he came back to see more of me each week. I was not the power runner I became in college, but rather, a fancy runner. As a thirteen-year-old freshman I made first-string halfback; as a junior I averaged 15.1 yards per carry; by my senior year I stood six-feet-one (only an inch less than my present height) and weighed two hundred pounds and was averaging 14.9 yards each trip with the ball. In basketball I set a Long Island high school record by scoring fifty-three points in one game and broke it the following week with fifty-five points. I averaged thirty-eight points as a senior. I starred for the lacrosse team. In short, I interested this recruiter named Kenneth Molloy.

Kenneth Molloy, attorney-at-law, was no buffoon of an alumnus. Ask him today why he chases around after high school athletes and he will tell you, "Aw, it's just something to get me out of the office." But the real reason this little Irish lawyer recruits athletes is that he gets a kick out of taking a punk kid by the scruff of the neck and making a successful man of him. Syracuse is Kenneth Molloy's alma mater, yet his recruits have been scattered all over the East. When he sees a kid who is not quite talented enough to play Syracuse's big-time athletics, he breaks his neck to get the kid a grant-in-aid from a school that plays sports a notch lower. He is a one-man college placement center and has a sharp eye for talent.

Since my teens, Kenneth Molloy has been that very special type of friend–the one who is there when you need someone. The time and effort he poured into the betterment of Jim Brown were considerable. As a youngster, whenever I had a problem I dropped by his office unannounced. Never was I told to come back later. He literally put aside his law practice for me, and in later years he handled legal matters for me without charge. The only fee he asks is that the kids he recruits go on to make something of themselves.

I had offers from forty-five colleges. My fifteen-yard rushing average and thirty-eight-point basketball average stimulated interest among all sorts of colleges. If I had chosen to, I could have played in the high-powered Big Ten conference, or if my preference had been the Ivy League I could have played there. One would suppose that Kenneth Molloy would have had no trouble persuading Syracuse to take me on. Yet such was not the case.

Strange and baffling developments–developments that eventually almost shattered my football career–began to unfold.

CHAPTER 3

"Don't be like Marion Farris"

Nobody can ever accuse me of having accepted an under-the-table deal when it came time to choose my college. I'm clean as a whistle on that score. With forty-five offers thrown in my lap, I chose to enroll at a school that was not interested in me. Talk about going where you're not wanted, I took the prize in that department.

The football public for years has assumed that I began college the usual way—on a free ride. Until now, I have never bothered to set the record straight, probably because nobody has asked me. I believe, however, that my story bears telling, for it may impress upon our universities and their coaches—particularly those in the South who inevitably must accept Negro athletes—the importance of judging each individual on his merits.

In the summer of 1953 I was still trying to make up my mind where to enroll. I'd left it to Ed Walsh, my Manhasset high school coach, to screen the offers, because I had complete faith in him. Woody Hayes wanted me at Ohio State, and Ed thought that was the place to go. "You have a special talent," he told me. "Ohio State is a good university and what's more, it's in the Big Ten, which plays the highest caliber of college football in the country. I think you ought to play with and against the best."

On the other hand, Kenneth Molloy, the Manhasset attorney

and Syracuse alumnus, argued for Syracuse. And in the process, he told me a little white lie. He told me Syracuse wanted me and had authorized him to offer me an athletic scholarship.

"Syracuse is a coming football power," Molloy told me. "They've been building up their schedule and they'll be top-drawer any day now. They have a fine curriculum and they offer a good social life for students. And this is important, Jimmy—you'll be fairly close to home. If you run into any serious problems at Syracuse, I'll be able to run up there and talk them over with you."

Molloy's last point sold me. Ohio State seemed like the other side of the country to me. I'd never been in the Midwest. I'd been handed around from St. Simons Island to Long Island and from my mother's sleep-in room to a foster home and then back to my mother again. The prospect of being yanked up again and deposited way out in Columbus with no friends worried me. So I chose Syracuse, and Kenneth Molloy got in touch with the Syracuse coaches and told them I was coming. He probably ruined their day.

What I did not know was that Molloy and a group of Manhasset citizens were going to pay my way.

I had no knowledge of a letter that Molloy sent to business and professional men and public officials in the community. It read:

You were undoubtedly one of those who felt pretty proud of Jimmy Brown and his athletic record at Manhasset High School. When he finished last June, he was probably Nassau County's outstanding athlete of all time.

There was good reason for our pride in this fine young American —and there will be more. But we need your help. That is, Jimmy Brown needs it. Here is the situation:

Jimmy recently matriculated at Syracuse University. When he did this, he relied upon the assurance of certain residents of Manhasset that they would contribute toward his expenses there. [Another little white lie—I knew nothing of any plans to assist me.] Frankly, Jimmy and his family cannot handle that, for it will come to about $1000 for this semester.

Given this chance, however, Jimmy will, we are convinced, give us in Manhasset ample reason to continue our confidence in him as an athlete and as a representative of all that is fine in young American manhood.

Several of us have joined to see what can be done to give Jimmy Brown his big chance. We think this will be one of Manhasset's soundest investments.

We think, too, that you may feel the same way about this or you would not have gotten this letter. If you agree, please send us your check to the order of Arthur H. Wright—as generous as you can make it—in the enclosed envelope.

Sincerely yours,
Kenneth D. Molloy

Forty-four men—an assortment ranging from Ernest G. Blaich, the local bank president, to Pete Sibell and Jack Bergstrom, who operated gas stations, and Karl Prewein, the Village Clerk—responded to Kenneth Molloy's letter. Once again, good people were going out of their way to help me. They thought I had potential as an athlete and human being, and they wanted me to be close enough that they could keep an eye on me. To no avail Molloy had pleaded with Syracuse to give me an athletic scholarship. "I cannot overemphasize this boy's potential in all sports," he'd written to one assistant football coach. But he was told: "The best we can offer is that if the kid comes here and makes the squad we'll give him a grant-in-aid in January when we cut the buck."

In January a few players usually drop out of school or flunk out; thus the coaches are able to distribute the dropouts' grants to new prospects. In the jargon of coaches, this is known as cutting the buck. Kenneth Molloy, deciding to get up a pot for my first-semester bills, was confident that I would quickly prove myself worthy of a piece of Syracuse's athletic buck.

At the same time, he knew that if he told me about his benevolent scheme I'd turn away from Syracuse instantly. If I knew that the Syracuse coaches were not interested in me, how could I be expected to go out for the team with any confidence in myself? And why would I want to take a one-semester screen-test at Syracuse when dozens of other schools were more than willing to accept me as bona fide college football material?

So Kenneth Molloy kept me in the dark. The day I left for college he even scrounged up a one-man committee to give me a VIP reception at the Syracuse airport. He telephoned upstate to an old friend, Arnie Burdick, who was then the Syracuse publicist but today is Sports Editor of the Syracuse *Herald-Journal,* and asked him to meet me. I felt like a big-time athlete stepping off the plane.

But so far as I know, the Syracuse coaches had never even scouted me in high school. It was true that the university was shooting for the big time, but Coach Ben Schwartzwalder and his assistants had been concentrating their scouting in the Pennsylvania coal fields (as what school didn't?). They had paid little or no attention to Long Island. To the best of my knowledge, even my fifteen-yard rushing average had not lured them to the scene. No doubt they had a very good reason for not beating a path to my door.

There was an athlete I shall fictitiously call Marion Farris who went to Syracuse and within a few years became a campus legend. I have heard many persons at Syracuse say that he was a terrific person. I have also heard others say less of him.

They said that he was the greatest lover who ever walked the Syracuse campus.

They said that he was a smooth talker who could lead others by the nose.

They said that coeds washed his argyle socks for him—that he never had to do his own laundry.

They said that he once got into a dispute with one of the coaches and punched him.

They said that coeds came out to the stadium and sang to him while he practiced.

And here was the real rub: He dated a lot of those coeds who washed his argyle socks and sang to him at the stadium.

Almost from the day I set foot on the Syracuse campus I heard one recurring theme: *"Don't be like Marion Farris."* Before long, I had those words ringing in my ears. "Don't be like Marion Farris," said Les Dye, the freshman football coach. "Don't be like Marion Farris," Ben Schwartzwalder eventually got around to saying. At every turn I got the same advice. Yet, I never heard any of the other players being told this. "Why tell me that?" I thought. "Just because I happen to be a Negro?"

I was the only Negro on the football squad. There seemed to be an assumption that I had come to Syracuse for no other reason than to be footloose and fancy-free. I had no idea whether Marion Farris had been a villain or a campus hero (remember, many students praised him), but one thing I did know was the fact that I was James Nathaniel Brown, not Marion Farris. I had come to Syracuse to get an education and play sports. I had not come to date white girls. I was even willing to wash my own socks. So why pick on me?

It seemed to me that everything was upside-down at Syracuse. In high school I had known nothing but fair treatment. Now I had advanced to the world of higher education and I felt that I had promptly been viewed as a potential troublemaker and threat to Caucasian women. Naturally enough, I got my back up. I bristled. I hadn't come to Syracuse to be treated like an enemy in the ranks.

Meanwhile, I was unpleasantly surprised to learn that I was to be a part of the freshman football squad only while on the practice field. The university in those days was growing by leaps and bounds, bursting at the seams, and was a mishmash of rising new dormitories and clutches of quonset huts left over from the war when Army Air Force men were stationed on campus. Athletes lived in a quonset hut area called Collendale, but I alone was assigned to live in another quonset hut area called Skytop, which lay high atop a hill by a ski lodge, about four or five miles from campus.

Non-athlete freshmen were quartered at Skytop, and it puzzled me that I wasn't rooming with the football players at Collendale, yet I didn't make an issue of it because I didn't mind Skytop. We had to hitch-hike to classes from Skytop, but I didn't mind that either. Besides, I liked my fellow freshmen and felt that I was benefiting from the oppportunity to associate with students other than football players. Skytop was good enough for me.

All my teammates were given meal tickets that entitled them to eighteen dollars' worth of meals per week. They ate in Slocum Hall, where the meat came thick and the gravy flowed. Non-athlete students who paid room and board fees were issued twelve-dollar tickets and ate in Sims Hall, where the food was okay but not sufficient for a growing football player. I was a big boy who practiced football every day, and I longed for those heaping portions they served at Slocum Hall. What was Syracuse trying to do, train me down to a chess player?

"Hey, I thought you were a football player," students would say to me at dinner. "How come you don't eat with the team?" I didn't know why. I figured maybe it was because if I got to eat a big meal I'd have enough strength to go out and chase white girls. Of course, I had no idea I was not on an athletic scholarship, nor was I to learn how I got into the university until after I graduated.

My first semester at Syracuse was not entirely a nightmare. During my hours away from athletics, life was largely all right. The students–unlike some of the faculty and coaches–did not seem to regard me as a Black Menace. They were friendly and completely natural with me. I was invited to pledge three fraternities and chose Pi Lambda Phi, a predominantly Jewish frat whose members had seemed to be the most fun. In some quarters, I imagine, people were saying, "I told you so." Marion Farris, you see, had been a Pi Lam.

I never did become a full-fledged fraternity brother. Ben Schwartzwalder told me, "I think you ought to quit that fraternity. It takes up too much of your time and distracts you from football." I was surprised. I hadn't suspected he cared.

Shut off from the football players' dormitories and from their dining hall, I circulated among other students and one day ran into a fellow named Vinnie Cohen from Brooklyn. He was related to very few of the legions of Brooklyn Cohens, for Vinnie, you see, was a Negro.

"Do you play basketball at all?" I asked him by way of idle conversation. He said, "I play a little. I'm not very good but I play some. Want to go up to the outdoor court at Skytop and play a little one-on-one?" I looked Vinnie Cohen over and saw that he was no more than six-feet-one. He had a slight pot belly and slumping posture. I thought, "This guy can't play basketball but I'll go up there and fool around with him anyhow." I was fairly proud of my basketball ability; in fact, I considered myself a better basketball prospect than football prospect.

Well, I soon found myself in a dogfight. Vinnie Cohen could jump out of this world. He could shoot and dribble like a magician. Right then, I made a promise to myself. "I'll never underestimate anybody again," I told myself. Vinnie and I became fast friends and roommates. He went on to score more points than any Syracuse player before him or since, and later became a staff attorney for the U. S. Department of Justice. At the time I first met him he was merely hoping to make the Syracuse team. Like myself, he had no athletic scholarship. Syracuse recruiters were doing a great job of spotting talent.

Unaware that I stood no higher than, say, an intramural league star who had gotten the notion he could make the university football squad, I reported for football and drew my uniform. "Come on, big Jim," said a slender, white-haired man. "Let's put on that uniform and get out there and see what you can do." The man who spoke was Roy Simmons, varsity backfield coach—the only encouraging voice I was to hear for a considerable while. Simmy alone seemed to regard me with an open mind, but unfortunately he worked little with the frosh squad.

Frosh coach Les Dye did no cartwheels when I showed up. "I don't know if we need halfbacks," he said. "We need ends, that's what we need." The thought crossed my mind that Dye did not regard my arrival as a banner day in Syracuse history. Be that as it may, I took the field with the other freshmen and participated in sprints. I outraced every man on the squad. "I didn't know you could run so fast," said Dye, whose filing cabinet obviously was not stuffed with scouting reports on me. "Maybe you'll be all right." I was encouraged. I remained a halfback.

From the beginning, it seemed crystal clear to me that the Syracuse coaching staff had little or no interest in me. I'm no mind reader, so it's possible I was wrong in concluding that the coaches regarded me as excess baggage, but the fact remains that the atmosphere in practice was so discouraging as to be crushing. To be sure, I received instruction: "Don't be like Marion Farris." But largely, I was ignored.

Perhaps I should have striven all the harder to make an impression, but I did not. My feeling was that coaches were supposed to evoke, not provoke, talent. Given an equal chance and the normal words of encouragement, I would have worked as hard as any man on the squad. But finding myself to be a *black* sheep from the outset, I quickly became surly, lackadaisical, and even inept. In the one frosh game in which Les Dye played me considerably, I showed nothing.

Our frosh squad had only a three-game schedule and concentrated more on absorbing Ben Schwartzwalder's varsity system than on winning. Mostly, we practiced—sometimes by ourselves, often with the varsity. Had the coaches bawled me out for my mistakes, at least I would have known why I seemed lost in the shuffle, but nobody bawled me out. The trouble was, the coaches scarcely spoke to me. Aside from dry comments from Les Dye, I seemed hardly worth speaking to.

My morale hit rock bottom. One day in practice I was given absolutely nothing to do. Instead of watching the proceedings with my helmet in my hand, or instead of dropping to one knee and pretending to be at least mildly interested in the goings-on, I sprawled out on my back, paying no attention to the drills. If this was not an open act of defiance, it was surely the worst practice-field form imaginable. The coaches studied me; but even then, they said nothing. "Well," I told myself, "they're happy. I've given them one more thing to talk about." Marion Farris himself probably had never sprawled out on his back in practice.

I was not a complete washout my freshman season. I had size and speed, and I believe the coaches could not help noticing this. In spite of my feeling of total depression, I usually practiced as well as anyone else when given a chance. But I kept telling myself, "Get out of this place. They don't want you here." Worse, I reached the point where I said, "Maybe those coaches are right. Maybe I don't have it."

Kenneth Molloy came up from Manhasset and tried to soothe my feelings, telling me that I was probably just going through a period of adjustment. Dr. Raymond Collins, the Manhasset school superintendent, made a special trip to Syracuse to find out what the devil was wrong. He felt personally responsible for my welfare, because he'd been one of those who had urged me to go to Syracuse and had contributed toward my tuition. Now he sought out Andy Mogish, an assistant football coach, and asked what the trouble was. Give or take a few words, this was what Mogish told Dr. Collins: "We have a lot of good backs who can really run. If Jimmy Brown is going to make the grade in college ball he'll probably have to make it in the line."

Dr. Collins went away from Mogish boiling. He had taught

at Syracuse and had followed Syracuse football for thirty years and thought he knew something about the game. Still simmering from his talk with Mogish, he ran into an old friend, Professor Michael Sawyer of the Political Science Department, and barked: "It's incredible to me that these coaches can misjudge this boy we sent them. If Syracuse has ever had a better back than Jimmy Brown, I'd like those coaches to tell me *who!*" Dr. Collins was so angry that if he could have had his way, he probably would have sent Ben Schwartzwalder and his staff back to physical education school for a refresher course in coaching.

I visited him in his room at the Onondaga Hotel. He looked nettled but was trying to restrain himself. He told me the gist of what Mogish had said about me but I sensed that Dr. Collins didn't want to say anything more–that he didn't want to belittle authority in my presence. "I don't know what to do, Dr. Collins," I said. "I can't seem to please these people. Maybe I just don't have it." "No, no. Stick it out," he said. "Study hard and keep your grades up. It's too soon to quit. If they keep giving you a bad deal after you've put in, say, a year, then we'll talk about arranging a transfer to Ohio State or somewhere."

"Well, I don't know," was all I could say.

The basketball season was coming on, and I figured things might take a turn for the better in that sport. So I decided to stay on. Along with Vinnie Cohen, I went out for freshman basketball. But the frosh basketball team, as it happened, was in the hands of one of my warmest admirers–Andy Mogish. (Mogish, I later learned, had told Dr. Collins, "I don't think Brown can fit in with the basketball team." And Collins had replied, "All he did was break all the Long Island scoring records.") Mogish, according to campus talk, was the coach that Marion Farris had punched. He did not tell me, "Don't be like Marion Farris." But I believe he felt that Jimmy Brown and Marion Farris were one and the same.

I scored a lot of points and grabbed a lot of rebounds for the freshman team, but I had to do it coming off the bench. Not until our eleventh game did I get a chance to start, and even after that I was only a sometime starter. We had a crack frosh team that won fourteen games and lost only one, but I didn't feel outclassed by the first-stringers. Before the season ended, both Vinnie Cohen and I broke the frosh scoring record. Considering that I'd done this while a substitute, I felt that at least in basketball, if not football, I had proven I was college material.

Yet January had come and gone, and the athletic department had not seen fit to cut me in for a piece of the athletic buck. Although at this time I remained unaware of the facts, the folks back in Manhasset were still paying my way through Syracuse, still hoping to convince Ben Schwartzwalder and his staff that I was the equal of their scholarshiped white sheep. I suspect the coaches were sick and tired of hearing from my Manhasset boosters and wished they'd keep their noses out of Syracuse business.

Meanwhile, winter turned to spring. At the time, Syracuse did not conduct spring football practice, so I decided to have a go at one more sport—track and field. I could sprint, hurl the discus, put the shot, high jump, and broad jump. I hoped that Bob Grieve, the track coach, would not hold Marion Farris against me. He did not. He welcomed me with open arms. He was downright sweet to me.

Grieve, it so happened, had about three scholarships a year to hand out—just enough to get a few good distance men and build a topflight two-mile relay team. Aside from them, poor Bob had to rummage through the student body, pep-talking anyone who was fast enough to catch a bus. He was forced to be a politician in order to collect a squad. He had to smile sweetly at guys who couldn't break eleven seconds in the hundred.

So, at last, I found a team whose coach did not tell me, "Don't be like Marion Farris." Bob Grieve would have grabbed Marion Farris.

As my first year at Syracuse was drawing to a close and summer vacation was coming on, Ben Schwartzwalder sent word to me to report to his office. Actually, I had not developed any strong resentment toward Schwartzwalder himself, for I knew that as head coach he had had to concentrate on the varsity and was forced to rely on his assistants for appraisals of me. Now, when I went to see him I found him sitting with Les Dye, the freshman coach.

"Les here thinks you can be a good end," Schwartzwalder told me. "I called you in because I want you to know what we expect of you next season. We need ends. I'd like you to go out for end."

"Coach, I don't want to go out for end," I said. "I've never played end. I don't particularly like end."

"Sometimes you have to do things for the good of the team," said Schwartzwalder. "Ray Perkins is a good halfback but he plays anywhere we want him to play. We needed ends last year, so he switched and did a good job for us."

"I still don't want to play end," I said.

Now Les Dye joined the conversation, appealing to my nobler instincts.

"You want to play pro ball, don't you?" he said. "In the pros, the ends and the quarterbacks make the most money, you know."

"I just don't want to play end," I said.

"Well," said Schwartzwalder, "we'll talk to you later."

A few days later he called me in and said, "I think we'll keep you at halfback." Looking back, I'm glad that I'd stuck to my guns. Ten seasons later in the National Football League, I almost doubled the so-called magic rushing figure of a thousand yards in one season, gaining 1863 yards in 1963. I might never have had the opportunity had I become an end at Syracuse. The thought makes me shudder.

CHAPTER 4

All hail Arthur Troilo!

"Practice punting," Kenneth Molloy told me when I arrived home for summer vacation in 1954. "If you can learn to punt you may be able to break into their lineup. They need a punter badly."

Okay, if a punter was what Syracuse needed I'd do my best to learn to punt. I resolved to think positively. If it was a gimmick I needed to break into the lineup, a gimmick I'd develop.

Molloy got me a summer job as a maintenance worker in the county park. It was a good job for a young fellow who had to practice punting. My duties were to go around the park picking up refuse and moving rocks from one place to another. There were not so many picnic leftovers or so many rocks as to interfere with my punting drills. The only trouble was, I couldn't learn to punt. I could placekick well enough, but my thighs just weren't built for punting. I'm heavily muscled in the thighs and as a result just don't have the fluid leg necessary for punting. I couldn't master the high, smooth follow-through.

"Well, just keep trying," said Molloy. "Meanwhile, you might also work on your shot putting and learn how to throw a javelin. The National AAU Decathlon Championships are in Atlantic City this summer. I'd like to see what you can do there."

For the benefit of those who don't follow track and field

closely, the decathlon is sport's greatest challenge. It is a fierce test of endurance and versatility in which the contestants run, jump, hurdle, vault, put the shot, hurl the javelin, throw the discus, and so on down the line. Strength, speed, stamina, and skill—all are required in this most grueling of all track and field endeavors. So I went to work practicing during working hours in the park, and practiced evenings at the high school field.

I'd never thrown a javelin, nor had I ever run the hurdles, nor had I ever pole vaulted. I had no coach to teach me, so I had to figure out the mechanics of these events on my own. I went to Atlantic City as the only self-taught decathlon contestant in the field.

When I arrived in Atlantic City, the town seemed to me to be a strange place to hold the National Decathlon. I wondered what the AAU moguls had been thinking when they chose Atlantic City. I had no track shoes, so right away I went out to buy a pair. But the city hosting the National Decathlon had no track store. Kenneth Molloy had to ship me a pair of shoes.

There were no courses for working out. We had to do our running on the beaches. Moreover, the site of the National Decathlon was a junky little stadium better suited for a softball game.

Still, I was thrilled to be entered. Great athletes were there. Rafer Johnson, who went on to win the Olympic decathlon championship, was there, a young fellow just starting out. Aubrey Lewis, an excellent athlete who went on to star in track and football for Notre Dame, was there. In all, some forty-five or fifty decathlon men—every one of them an all-around athlete—were in the field.

I botched up a few events but managed to finish tenth, which was pretty good for a guy who'd had no coaching. Placing high in a big-time athletic event was an experience that picked up my spirits and renewed my confidence. It improved my frame of mind for my return to Syracuse and another crack at making the grade in football. I promised Kenneth Molloy I would hustle like blazes regardless of how dim my chances looked.

By this time, Molloy had succeeded in getting me an athletic scholarship. I suppose the coaches had decided to take a chance on my size and speed. (Also, I had succeeded in getting through my first year at Syracuse without dating one white girl or recalling Marion Farris's transgressions.)

Upon arriving for preseason training, I entered the locker room and found that the coaches had posted a list that broke down the squad into probable units. They had me down for fifth-string left halfback. "Well, that's all right," I told myself. "I'll just go out and hustle like I told Kenneth Molloy I would."

Practicing under Schwartzwalder himself now, I came to like the man almost immediately. An ex-watchcharm lineman from West Virginia, he was short and stocky and wore glasses and had a fuzz of gray hair atop his round little owl-like head. Altogether, he looked like a grumpy museum guard. He had been a Silver Star paratrooper in the Normandy invasion, and it was said of him that he was so cool that he dozed off crossing the English Channel.

He was tough and sarcastic, but seemed fair. He taught sledgehammer football and was a bug on conditioning. Every day, after we had done calisthenics and then practiced for a couple of hours, we had to run three laps—almost a mile. We did not jog those laps—we *raced* them, and our order of finish was duly noted by Schwartzie. A distance race is a hard way to top off a scrimmage. Anyhow, I made up my mind that I would finish first—or at the worst, second—every day.

"Over my dead body," said a teammate named Dick Lasse.

Lasse was a regular Jack Armstrong. As I mentioned earlier, he later went on to pro ball in Pittsburgh but was horrified by the Steelers' disregard for strict rules of training. At Syracuse he was a big, fast end who came to camp in shape to take on a company of Marines.

After our first few days in camp, during which Lasse and I had dueled like wild men to win the races, our teammates came to us frowning and stated a proposition. It went like this:

"Look, we don't care if you guys win these damned races, but how about letting up on the pace, huh? You can fight it out in the home stretch."

"That suits me fine," I said. "I don't like this any more than you guys do."

"Nothing doing," said Lasse. They had as much chance of getting Lasse to run a dishonest race as they had of putting a fix in with the university chaplain.

Running laps against him almost killed me, but I always finished first or second. The two of us were always neck and neck at the finish. "Maybe Brown is ready to play some football," I could see the coaches thinking. They moved me up to second-string as the season drew near.

A guy named Sam Alexander was our first-string left halfback. I'm not belittling Sam when I say I thought I could carry the ball better than he. I was simply bigger and faster. But Sam was a senior and I was a sophomore, and there seemed to be an unwritten rule at the time that sophomores just didn't supplant seniors. All of our first-string backs were seniors. Well, at least I knew that Ben Schwartzwalder knew I was around, for he'd fetched me up from fifth-string to second. And then, a week before our opening game with Villanova, Sam Alexander suffered a leg injury in a scrimmage. Schwartzwalder promoted me to first team. I made up my mind that I would be fierce and quick in my debut.

On the very first offensive play of my career I fumbled. I wasn't even hit—I just dropped the ball. Schwartzie got me out of there so fast I probably left a stream of blue smoke behind me. He preferred to take his chances with Sam the cripple.

We beat Villanova rather handily, 28–6, and I did get to play somewhat, carrying the ball six more times and averaging almost seven yards per carry. But my star had descended the moment I'd committed that fumble. As the season progressed, I carried the ball from time to time but got a great deal more exercise playing defense.

Syracuse hadn't really become a college power yet, but our schedule now included a few rugged teams, and one was Illinois, our fourth opponent. As I recall, a rash of backfield injuries hit us the week of the Illinois game, so I moved back into the starting lineup. Though Illinois slaughtered us, 34–6, I averaged more than five yards on thirteen carries. On one play I raced around end for twenty yards before being stopped by J. C. Caroline, the All-American who now stars on the Chicago Bears defense. I smashed Caroline's shoulder and put him out of the game. But I made no smash hit with our coaches. I'd fumbled a kickoff, thereby giving them a chance to say, "He's a poor risk." Against Holy Cross the next week, I was back on the bench.

I kept hustling. Curiously, the fans and the school publicity man felt much more strongly than the coaching staff that I might look good in the Syracuse offense.

"We want Brown! We want Brown!" the fans chanted while I went along sitting on the bench. They made me feel good.

Arnie Burdick, the publicist, began slipping little boosts for Jimmy Brown into his press releases. I had a lobby plugging me at the Burdick home–Arnie's wife Joyce, who ran the young people's dances at the YWCA, kept telling him, "Jimmy Brown comes well dressed, has good manners, and brings the best phonograph records. He *must* be a good football player." Now if only I could get the coaches to think I could run with that ball!

Finally, I got my big break in the sixth game, against Cornell. Sam Alexander was on the injured list again. Now don't jump to premature conclusions–I didn't move up to Sam's job. As a matter of fact, the coaches maneuvered rather desperately to prevent my breaking into the starting lineup.

They switched Ray Perkins, our right halfback, to Alexander's left halfback post. A fellow named Arthur Troilo, our second-string right halfback, moved up to the first team. But the coaching staff's careful plans blew up early in the first quarter when Troilo suffered an ankle injury and had to leave the game. So now Perkins had to be shifted back to right half, and I entered the game at left half. What else could our coaches do?

I repaid their confidence in me by ripping off a fifty-four-yard touchdown run. We lost, 14–6, but I gained 151 yards and won a first-string job at last. Too bad the season had only two weeks to go.

In my first game as a starter, we played Colgate, our arch-rival. The Syracuse-Colgate game was always a festive affair preceded by a lot of good old-fashioned college pranks. Syracuse men would sneak into Ithaca and try to capture a Colgate man; if successful, they would scalp an S on his head with clippers. Colgate men tried to capture Syracuse men and scalp them with a C. In short, the Syracuse-Colgate game was the high point of the season, and here I was on the first team now.

In the dressing room before the game, a little blond-haired quarterback named Mickey Rich came up to me looking very intense. He proceeded to give me a pep talk. "Look, now," he said, "you're not like Farris, and you've got a chance to show them you're not." I went limp. Mickey Rich meant well, but whenever I got that Marion Farris routine or the you-can-be-a-credit-to-your-race routine, I always felt like an animal who was being tolerated in the living room as long as he didn't shed hair on the sofa. I looked at Mickey and said, "Okay," and let it go at that.

That day I scored touchdowns on runs of forty-one and seventeen yards and gained more than a hundred yards for the second straight week. We whipped Colgate, 31–12, and were on our way to becoming a college power. (Colgate later dropped us from their schedule.) I was on my way as a ball-carrier and now I was a campus celebrity.

Arthur Troilo's injury has always seemed to me the turning

point in my athletic career, and yet as I look back now, I know that the sky did not suddenly turn blue for me all at once. Syracuse coaches did not clasp me to their bosoms that quickly.

My next job was to convince Marc Guley, the varsity basketball coach, that I could play basketball. It wasn't easy.

The Monday after the football season ended I reported for basketball. Guley said later he'd been impressed by my promptness, because football players who double in basketball often loaf for a week or two before reporting. Impressed or not, he puzzled me. He gave no sign that he held Marion Farris against me, but for reasons I can't pin down he made no headlong rush to use me. I appeared doomed to be sixth man. In our tenth game I scored thirty-three points after he sent me into the game with only three minutes left in the first half. From then on, Guley started me. But I couldn't help thinking I could have played on the first team all along, because when the season ended and the statistics were compiled I was the team's leading rebounder and second-leading scorer.

I kept working as hard as I could. In the spring I lettered in track and field and in one meet, against Alfred College, scored twenty-eight points, a total which track experts equate with gaining perhaps 350 yards in a football game. The point is, I felt that by being an iron man I'd erase any lingering doubts that the athletic department might have about my seriousness of purpose. Now, with my sophomore year not quite over, I'd already made it big in three sports, and Syracuse was becoming a wonderful place. Arnie Burdick, the publicist, began beating the drums for me, labeling me a future All-American. I figured I'd been accepted, but I was due for a shock.

We opened the 1955 football season against Pittsburgh. Pitt was strong and deep and was to prove it that season by going all the way to the Sugar Bowl. The Pitt coach, John Michelosen, was noted for his bulldog defenses that smothered runners. He smothered me, all right. I gained only twenty-eight yards in twelve carries. And when I walked on the practice field the following Monday, I found myself demoted to second team. I turned right around and walked off the field. I went straight to the dressing room and began changing clothes.

Arnie Burdick had been watching practice. He followed me. "What's the matter? You're not hurt, are you?" he said.

"No, I'm not hurt," I told Arnie. "I'm fed up. I'm packing and getting out of this school."

"Now don't do anything rash until you've talked to Ken Molloy, Jim. It's the least you owe him."

I could not see how Molloy could say anything that would change the situation. I felt that I would always be the goat at Syracuse. Maybe it seems childish and petulant for me to have walked off the field because I had been demoted. Maybe Ben Schwartzwalder was merely testing the old psychology on me, reminding me that I didn't have it made. But I had spent two years—half of my college life—trying to overcome a prejudgment that stemmed from the coaching staff's dislike for another man. I figured Schwartzie for a fair man, and now, when he of all people put me down, I had to conclude that all my efforts had been wasted.

Arnie Burdick argued with me, and finally I agreed to phone Ken Molloy. He convinced me to stay—that I would be throwing two years out the window if I left now. I went back to my second-string job the next day, but I was on fire inside.

Burdick, of course, was there, standing on the sidelines with just a trace of a grin at the corner of his mouth. That afternoon, says Arnie today, "Jim gave the greatest performance I ever saw him render. Playing with the seconds, he just bowled over the varsity. What a carnage."

I don't know about carnage, but I left a few tacklers stretched. In five plays I ran for four touchdowns.

Schwartzie put me back on the first team to stay.

At last the coaches accepted me, as students had done from

the beginning. Now I had everything and everybody going for me. And the result was that I became something of a jerk.

If I've seemed a little hard on the Syracuse coaches in these pages, it's time I put the scales in balance. I feel within my heart that once they accepted me they were men enough to recognize that they had been guilty of twisted thinking. I am certain that their acceptance of me was something more than simply saying, "He'll win games for us, so we may as well use him." I believe they made up their minds to be fair men, and as a result Syracuse became one of the best places for a Negro athlete to enroll. From time to time during my career in pro ball, I've run into Les Dye, the coach who wanted to make me an end. When he sees me he's kind and polite and, I suspect, a little embarrassed. And as we talk I'm always a little embarrassed for Les, because I'm sure he realizes he made a mistake, and I realize that every man has a right to make mistakes. Which brings me to the fact that while the Syracuse coaches may have done me wrong for a while, I did myself an injustice at a time when I had no excuse for it.

I became a goof-off. Having at last won a first-string football berth, I lost sight of the fact that being a star athlete does not excuse a man from amounting to something as a person. In sports I competed with all the determination at my command, yet all the while, a disturbing change was taking place in me.

I was beginning to study only as hard as I had to—only hard enough to maintain the C average that was necessary to remain eligible for sports. I was, as they say, beating the system. Furthermore, I began ducking the phases of college life that I found unpleasant. One such phase was ROTC (Reserve Officers Training Corps). A man named Colonel Ernest L. Meggs was in charge of ROTC, and as I was soon to learn, Colonel Meggs was a most unusual man.

I had gone into ROTC in my freshman year when the entire frosh football squad was advised to sign up or risk being drafted. From the day we were issued uniforms I disliked ROTC intensely.

I disliked it because the Corps was something considerably less than Abercrombie & Fitch when it came to fitting a man out.

I was a large man, and there was no uniform left that fit me. My coat was too small. My wrists dangled from my sleeves. My waist belt circled my body just below the vicinity of my chest. My trousers left a clear view of my ankles and then some. My shoes, on the other hand, were too large. They flapped when I walked. I don't recall what make they were, but probably they had been custom-made for Ringling Brothers.

When I put on that uniform I felt mortified. My mother had instilled in me an insistence on good appearance. Now I had to go out and drill on the campus quad; as it was, I stood head and shoulders above the men in the ranks, and with my ill-fitting uniform adding the perfect touch I felt like a clown. Students gathered around to watch. I could almost hear them giggling.

I went into my junior year still cursed with that same uniform, but by this time I'd begun to cut drills whenever I could get away with it and frequently when I did show up for drills I came in street clothes. "My uniform's at the tailor's," I'd say. Of course, it wasn't. The tailor would have had to start from scratch with a fresh bolt of cloth.

Soon I got orders to report to Colonel Meggs's office.

"This is it," I told myself. "Here's where I get bounced out."

I could picture the scene. Meggs was a tough officer who each summer went to Fort Bragg, North Carolina, to drill advanced ROTC men and each year won the "best company" award. He was a hard, hard soldier. I could just see him sitting behind his desk and slapping my record in front of me. He would recite all my sins, bawl me out, and then read me out of the Corps. I expected nothing less. I put on my surliest face and reported to his office.

"Look here," Colonel Meggs began. "I know all about your record. It's terrible. But I think you can be a fine officer, a real good lieutenant. I think you have much more ability than a lot of men out there, but you're not applying yourself. I don't know why you're not, but whatever the reason is, I don't want to kick you out.

"If you just buckle down," the colonel went on, "you will be one of the top officers in this doggone Corps."

I was stupefied, to put it mildly. I said to myself:

"Look at this guy! I'm supposed to get bounced out and he sits there talking to me like *this!*"

"You know I can kick you out right here and now," Colonel Meggs said, "but what I want you to do is when the time comes for you to take your six weeks at Fort Bragg this summer, work hard down there and show all these men you can be a good officer."

Not once did the colonel ask me why I'd goofed off. Truly, if he had asked me, I doubt that I would have told him about the uniform. More likely, I would have given him some lame lies. I think he knew that. He wasn't going to give me a chance to make an ass of myself. He wasn't interested in painting me into a corner where I would make excuses. He knew, all right, that there had to be reasons for my poor record, but the reasons weren't nearly as important to him as how I *ought* to be conducting myself. In a word, he understood.

In effect he was saying, "Let's start here–let's start all over and do a job. I'm giving you the chance."

I walked out of the colonel's office and said to myself, "If he thinks I can be a good officer I'm certainly going to give it a try." In the space of a few minutes, Colonel Ernest L. Meggs had become Ed Walsh, Jay Stranahan, Patrolman Jack Peploe, Kenneth Molloy, and Dr. Raymond Collins all rolled into one. He knew his job was not merely to keep young people in line, but rather to get something out of them, and to bend over backwards to do it if necessary.

I went out and marched my tail off in that silly uniform, even though I thought my tail would burst right through it at any moment. I went down to Fort Bragg and was cited as the top cadet in my platoon. Later, I went on to earn my commission, and I am to this day eager to say that while the Army (and Army officers, specifically) frequently are held up to ridicule, I am impressed with the Army (and with Army officers, specifically). Some of the best men I've seen have been officers. There is an integrity about them; they are opposed to excuses and in favor of accepting responsibility. If a man serves under a good officer and does not carry away at least a little brick and mortar for the building of his philosophy, he has let something of value slip from his fingers.

Colonel Meggs did more than make an officer of me. He made me take a good look at myself. "Here's a man who gave me a break when I didn't deserve a break," I told myself. "Now where do I go from here?"

Where I had been content to eke out a C average by the skin of my teeth, just to stay eligible for sports, I now pushed up my grades. No candidate for *cum laude* was I, but I began earning C-plus and B-minus grades. In athletics, of course, I continued to make progress, but more important, my place on the Syracuse scene meant more to me now because I was able to appreciate the spirit and purpose of the university. Although physical education was my major, the philosophy of logic became my favorite study. It formed the cornerstone of what has been my philosophy in adult life—namely, that nothing is entirely black or entirely white and that when a man loses sight of this he can no longer tell truth from falsehood or right from wrong.

Colonel Meggs made Jim Brown the student buckle down, and Ben Schwartzwalder saw to it that Jim Brown the athlete never let up. Like the colonel, Schwartzie was a tough drillmaster.

"Drop that shoulder! Level when you go in there, Flash! Level, level, level!"

Level was probably Schwartzie's favorite word. He taught hard-nosed football. Even though I had proved myself an asset to his offense, I was still a fancy Dan. I gave tacklers the cross-over step—the left-leg-over-the-right-leg manuever you see halfbacks making in posed photographs. A guy could get himself broken in half doing that.

"Level, level, level!"

Schwartzie meant to make a hard-nosed ball carrier of me, and if it took sarcasm (Flash) he had plenty to offer. He was doing a good job.

In my junior year I finished second only to Penn State's Lenny Moore among the East's top rushers. My senior year I set a national record by scoring forty-three points against Colgate, but Colgate by this time was out of its class playing us. Pittsburgh once again stopped me cold and beat us, but that was the only regular-season game we lost. We defeated powerful teams. I rolled for 154 yards against Maryland, which had gone undefeated the previous season. I gained 125 yards and scored the game's only touchdown in a victory over Army. I consistently gained more than a hundred yards a game, but I had the strong support of able teammates, for Schwartzie had fashioned his powerhouse at last and made it hard-nosed.

It sounds trite and perhaps insincere to say that I owed much of my football success to teammates, but to cite only one example, how could I overlook the likes of Jim Ridlon, the right halfback who was my running mate?

"Jimmy Brown gets so much credit," some people observed, "that Jim Ridlon doesn't get enough."

Ridlon, who later went on to the San Francisco 49ers as a defensive back, was a fine running back who kept the defense honest, preventing them from ganging up on me. He was an artist and sculptor, and proposed to do a bust of me. He wanted the campus to have something to remember me by. Our athletic department nixed the bust because busts had not been made of past Syracuse stars, but the mere fact that Jim had proposed to sculpt a remembrance of the guy who kept him in the shadows indicated why we were a fine football team.

The Cotton Bowl was studying us as a possible opponent for

Texas Christian, but the bowl committee was not enthusiastic. In 1952, after enjoying a brief taste of football success, Syracuse had gone to the Orange Bowl and been humiliated by Alabama, 61–6. In view of that result, and in view of the fact that eastern football was sniffed at in many quarters, the Dallas people regarded us as a risk. They hesitated right up till our final game with Colgate.

The week of the Colgate game, our players held a meeting and decided to beat the devil out of poor little Colgate. We laid it on, 61–7. The bowl bid was ours.

Once the invitation came, many persons wondered how I, a Negro, would be treated in Dallas and in the game itself. I worried a little myself. I was the only Negro on our squad and was afraid the school would tell me I'd have to live apart from the team. I made up my mind that if it came to that, I'd say, "I'm not going."

Meanwhile, I went to New York to appear with the All-American team on the Ed Sullivan show. While there, I met two Texas Christian players, Ken Wineburg and Norm Hamilton. They were perfectly cordial to me. My only complaint was that Ed Sullivan made us come out in football uniforms and sneakers (so we wouldn't scratch the stage). I didn't know whether to grunt or do a pirouette.

Meanwhile, back at the campus, Syracuse officials were laying travel plans. They told me nothing, which was exactly the right thing to do because they had no intention of segregating me and thought it unnecessary even to tell me they wouldn't. I stayed with the team in a nice hotel in a Dallas suburb and went along with the team to a downtown movie house. I suppose the theater was segregated, but I sat downstairs with my teammates.

Many people expected the T.C.U. players to give me a hard time in the Cotton Bowl. It was anticipated that at the very least I would be called foul names in every pileup. Nothing of the sort happened. The T.C.U. players hit me hard but never dirty. They even helped me to my feet. They called me no names. In the years since, I've read that Abe Martin, the T.C.U. coach, has always been as interested in teaching character as in winning games. I believe it, for I suspect that the T.C.U. team I played against was a reflection of Abe Martin's own character.

Anyhow, thanks to as weird a circumstance as ever decided a bowl game, we lost to T.C.U., 28–27.

Following our third touchdown, I dropped back to kick the extra point. Just as our team was lining up, our fullback decided to exchange blocking assignments with one of our ends. The two players fell to discussing the switch. Meanwhile, our center set himself to snap the ball. On extra point attempts we had no hike signal; the center could snap the ball as soon as he felt comfortable. Unaware that two of our men were discussing blocking assignments, he snapped the football. Right through the discussion flew a T.C.U. player named Chico Mendoza. He came in untouched and blocked my kick. The strange thing was that he rushed in so fast that if I had stopped kicking he would have run past me and I would have been able to start over and kick the point.

In any case, even though we lost the game we had given such a good account of ourselves that we were welcomed back to Syracuse like victors. I myself profited hugely from my experience in Dallas. Although I was an All-American, I had had no real national reputation prior to the Cotton Bowl game, largely because eastern football was still lightly regarded. But in the bowl game I scored twenty-one of the Syracuse points and was named the game's Most Outstanding Player. Millions had seen the game on TV. Many Texans sent me kind letters complimenting me on my performance. And, of course, my bargaining position versus the Cleveland Browns was strengthened overnight.

My last days at Syracuse were great fun and enormously satisfying. In lacrosse–my favorite sport–I tied Jack Daut of Rutgers for the national scoring championship and made All-American.

In the annual North-South all-star game at Baltimore I scored five goals and had two assists though playing only half the game.

"Brown is the greatest lacrosse player I've ever seen," said Gardner Mallonee, the former Johns Hopkins All-American and coach. Charley Clarke, president of the U. S. Intercollegiate Lacrosse Association, said of me, "I've never seen a better lacrosse player." Such words may have been extravagant but I treasure them, for I always loved lacrosse and tried to give it everything I had.

More schools ought to take up this old Indian sport. It's sort of a cross between field hockey and football. The guy with the little white ball is fair game for tacklers and must whirl and dodge for his life. The reason I liked lacrosse better than football was that lacrosse practice was fun, whereas football practice was hard work. I had a great coach, Roy Simmons, who in his other capacity as assistant football coach had been the only member of Ben Schwartzwalder's staff to encourage me from the beginning.

In my senior year, Arnie Burdick, my good and faithful drumbeater, moved over to the Sports Editor's desk at the *Herald-Journal,* and was succeeded by Val Pinchbeck, an equally energetic press agent who is fond of recalling my very last day in a Syracuse uniform. From the window of his publicity office, he spied on me and caught me in a moment of sentimentality. Later he told a reporter for *Sport* Magazine:

"We had a track and lacrosse doubleheader against Army at Archbold Stadium that day, and 7500 people turned out to see Jim's last performance as a Syracuse athlete. He scored thirteen points in the track meet, then changed uniforms and led the lacrosse team to a victory that gave us an undefeated season. I watched all this and then went back to my office, and a while later I looked out on the empty stadium and saw Jim come out of the dressing room alone.

"He was carrying his duffel bag and walking slowly across the field, as if he hated to leave. He climbed to the top row of the stadium and then turned around and stood there looking the place over. There wasn't a soul around.

"I kept watching Jim, and then I saw him wave gently to the old stadium and then turn around and leave. I said to myself, 'Well, I guess that guy got something out of his four years here.'"

Val Pinchbeck was right–I had gotten something very special from Syracuse. I had learned a mighty important lesson.

When I waved goodbye to Archbold Stadium I knew that I would always remember there is no substitute for hard work. Standing there, I could hardly believe that I had become an All-American, for only a few years earlier I had been as far down as an athlete could be. I had come from nothing to something, and now I realized that having to fight my way up was the greatest experience I could have had.

In my freshman year I had actually lost confidence in my ability. I had almost packed my bags. If I hadn't stuck it out, if good people hadn't encouraged me, I would have been in trouble for the rest of my life. I probably would have formed a cynical philosophy wherein I just wouldn't believe in anything or anybody. But thanks to the people who prodded me, I had come back in my sophomore year running and hustling and sticking with it, and the pieces started falling in place. I learned to have faith in the future, and as I left Syracuse I told myself:

"Maybe you can't see what lies ahead two or three or four years from now, but if you work hard and have the right attitude things will work out for the best. When things don't go smoothly, just lay in there and something will break."

Actually, my very last appearance in Archbold Stadium was not as an athlete but as a member of the graduating class. The faculty named me class marshal for the School of Education, and I led our class in the procession. I wore no cap and gown, but rather a summer ROTC uniform (this one fit!), for I was to receive my lieutenant's bars. All the pieces had fallen into place.

Looking back, I'm glad Marion Farris had made a few people

angry enough to take it out on me. If I had been a big shot from the very start, I might have gone straight down to nothing instead of coming up to something. Or I might not have learned that when a man is down, there are people who come along to help out. By nature I am somewhat of a skeptic—I've seen so much incompetence and dishonesty and blindness that I tend to be leery of people until I have seen proof that they're good and honest. But a man must believe in the human race if he is to be a decent person himself. Colonel Meggs, the hard soldier . . . Kenneth Molloy, the interested alumnus . . . Roy Simmons, the kindly backfield coach . . . Schwartzie, the hard-driving but fair boss . . . Jim Ridlon, the selfless teammate . . . these were the people at Syracuse who represented goodness and honesty.

So without hesitation I was able to urge Ernie Davis to enroll at Syracuse. And now I must speak at length of Ernie Davis, because he was the most courageous man I have ever known.

CHAPTER 5

Embarrassed to die

Ernie Davis lies buried in Woodlawn Cemetery, Elmira, New York. Not far from his grave is the resting place of Samuel Langhorne Clemens, Mark Twain, who once penned words that suggest something of the Ernie Davis I knew.

"Your true pilot," Mark Twain wrote, "cares nothing about anything on earth but the river, and his pride in his occupation surpasses the pride of kings."

Ernie Davis took great pride in an occupation he never got a chance to pursue. He was pure football player. With Ernie, the game was the thing. When he chose his college the question that worried him was, would that college play enough topflight teams to give his ability a true test? When the time came for him to turn pro he gave no thought to entering any but the toughest league, the N.F.L. He was relieved when Washington traded its draft claim on him to Cleveland. His feeling of relief had nothing to do with the fact that Washington clubowner George Preston Marshall previously had not seen fit to employ a Negro player. Ernie couldn't have cared less about that. He simply wanted to play for a strong club, and Cleveland was stronger than Washington.

Though the most publicized college star in the nation, he would have taken the first offer Cleveland made him had not Tony De-

Filippo, an Elmira attorney, restrained him. Tony was friend and counselor and substitute father to fatherless Ernie, and yet Tony had no easy job negotiating for Ernie. Tony insisted on time to make an exhaustive study of pro football's financial structure in order to determine Ernie's worth. All the while, Ernie itched to sign, for he was a gentle man who simply assumed he would be treated fairly. In an age when college stars dicker like bankers, Ernie never lost sight of the fact that money is not the only satisfaction in being a pro.

"Some people play for money or for other reasons," said John Brown, a tackle who moved along with Ernie from Syracuse to Cleveland. "Ernie wanted to play pro football just because he wanted to play. He loved it."

Ernie Davis died in public, which is a terribly hard way to die. The world knew, just as he himself knew, that the acute leukemia that sidelined him only days before he was to report to the Browns was incurable. Yet he was big and strong and the disease could not put him down, so he walked in the public eye for nine months. Whenever he signed his autograph he wrote: "Ernie Davis, Cleveland Browns, 1962."

This was, I suppose, his way of saying that it was important to him that he had come as far as he had, even if he would never play a game of pro ball. Sadly, his autograph read like an epitaph: ". . . Cleveland Browns, 1962." There was finality in it.

But Ernie wanted no pity. If he ever asked himself "Why me?" none of us knew. He never said it aloud, not even to his closest friends. He bore himself with such gentle dignity that men who knew him only briefly wept when the end came.

Afterward, Dr. Austin Weisberger, a noted hematologist who had treated Ernie, received a letter from a small boy. It read:

"I met Ernie Davis. He was so nice. I loved him. Here is twenty-five cents in his name to fight leukemia. I'll never forget him."

Most people mistakenly thought Ernie to be a quiet, almost withdrawn person. I suppose this was so because he was soft-spoken and had no gift for glibness among strangers. He was impeccably polite to fans, and always patient. In the company of friends, however, he was more at ease; though no jokester, he had a lively, appreciative sense of humor, and contributed thoughtfully to any intelligent discussion. In his handsome face there was sensitivity which, with no need of words, conveyed his goodness to strangers.

I first met Ernie in the spring of 1957, shortly before my graduation from Syracuse. Ben Schwartzwalder, the head football coach, had asked me to visit Ernie in Elmira and discuss the possibility of his enrolling at Syracuse. I was impressed the moment I met him.

I had thought that perhaps he would be one of those flashy high school stars who wore suede shoes, low-cut two-button suits, and shirts with flared collars. Actually, I found him exactly the opposite. He wore a tastefully conservative Ivy League suit and cordovan shoes. It was obvious that he concerned himself with good appearance.

Notre Dame wanted Ernie badly. But I had not gone to Elmira to sway him from Notre Dame or any other school. Our coaching staff felt that as a student I might be able to shed light on aspects of campus life with which adults had no familiarity. This I was willing to do. I would tell Ernie the good and the bad. He knew that I had been the only Negro on the football squad.

"How will they treat me?" he wanted to know. I told him all about my early experiences at Syracuse. I told him that I had had a bad time because some people had assumed that the presence of a Negro on the squad meant trouble. I told Ernie I had had a hard fight proving myself. "But that's why I think they'll treat you well," I said. "They know now that their attitude toward me was wrong. They're conscious now of the fact that they must treat everybody fairly."

I told Ernie that he would find a good social life at Syracuse but that football players had poor housing. "We're still living in those quonset huts the Air Force left behind from the war. In the winter the heat often goes off, and it gets so cold you hate to get up from under the blankets." I pointed out that the school was building new dorms but I had no idea when they would be ready. I told him if he wanted glamorous dorms, he should go elsewhere.

But mainly, Ernie wanted to know if I thought the schedules that Syracuse had booked would be tough enough for him to prove his mettle. The schedules had a few weak spots but I felt they were sufficiently tough. I was impressed by Ernie's desire to play against the best. Some may find it a paradox that he was a terribly fierce competitor and yet a touchingly gentle soul, but I think not. A friend recently showed me a paragraph written by A. J. Liebling when he was a war correspondent in 1943 England. Liebling's words make one think of Ernie:

"I knew that the quality of American troops would be good, once they had paid their entry fee with a couple of bobbles, because Americans are the best competitors on earth. A basketball game between two high-school teams at home will call forth enough hardness of soul and flexibility of ethic to win a minor war; the will to win in America is so strong it is painful, and it is unfettered by any of the polite flummery that goes with cricket. This ruthlessness always in stock is one of our great natural resources. It is better than the synthetic fascist kind, because the American kid wears it naturally, like his skin, and not self-consciously, like a Brown Shirt. Through long habit he has gained control over it, so that he turns it on for games, politics, and business and usually turns it off in intimacy. He doesn't have to be angry to compete well."*

Ernie Davis was never angry. Yet I felt on first meeting him that he could be fierce on the field. When I left him that day in Elmira, he did not tell me whether he intended to choose Syracuse, nor did I ask. Probably it was Tony DeFilippo, an alumnus of Syracuse, who in the end most influenced his choice. I know

The Most of A. J. Liebling, selected by William Cole (New York: Simon & Schuster, 1963).

that Ernie hesitated for a considerable time simply because he was wary of following in my footsteps. I had broken the records at Syracuse and become an All-American. Inevitably, I would be the yardstick by which people would measure Ernie. Would he be as good as Jim Brown? Would he be better? Did he want to be another Jim Brown? Ernie did not fear the comparisons. He simply wanted to make the grade on his own merits and in his own way.

He broke all my records and was the first Negro to win the Heisman Trophy, which goes annually to the most outstanding college football player in the nation. He led the graduation procession. In short, he accomplished all that he could have hoped for at Syracuse, and now he meant to show that he could be a pro in every sense of the word.

Although I tried to be of help to Ernie and Tony DeFilippo during negotiations with the Browns, I was not entirely happy with the prospect of playing alongside Ernie. I knew that Paul Brown planned to adopt Green Bay's so-called big back system, which is roughly a two-fullback system geared for strong emphasis on power. Like me, Ernie was big and fast. But I wasn't sold on the big-back system. I had been hoping that Paul would change his coaching methods, but was the big-back system the right answer? I believed in a balanced attack. I did not say to myself, "The big-back system won't work for us," but I was skeptical. I'll never know, of course, whether the system would have worked.

In August 1962, Ernie reported to the College All-Stars, who were to meet the Green Bay Packers, champions of the N.F.L., in Chicago. A few days before the game he developed symptoms that required examination. At Evanston General Hospital the doctors diagnosed his illness as leukemia and telephoned Art Modell. Modell and Tony DeFilippo rushed to Evanston.

The doctors, meanwhile, did not tell Ernie the nature of his illness. He thought it might be mumps or mononucleosis. He had been told only that he would not be able to play in the All-Star game. When Modell and DeFilippo entered his hospital room they found him sitting on the edge of the bed crying. This was the only time he lost his composure.

"He was bewildered, confused," Art Modell told me later. "He felt fine and wanted to play but was told he couldn't. He was unable to understand why." As I've said of Ernie before, the game was the thing.

I quickly received word that Ernie had leukemia. Modell and the doctors leveled with Ernie's close friends and sportswriters, asking them to keep the news out of the papers. The press reported simply and briefly that Ernie was under treatment for a "blood infection." Of course, the truth always leaks out in cases such as Ernie's, but the cover-up was worth a try.

The prognosis at Evanston was that Ernie had only a few months to live. Art Modell was badly shaken. I imagine you have to know Art to be as certain as I am that his concern for Ernie had nothing whatever to do with the fact that Ernie represented a small fortune gone down the drain. Having given up Bobby Mitchell and a first draft choice for the right to hand Ernie an eighty-thousand-dollar contract, Art's total loss amounted to hundreds of thousands in player property value. That kind of money carries a lot of meaning to Art, because he came into his money the hard way, starting as an electrician's helper at eighty-seven cents an hour. Yet more than anything else, Art is a compassionate man. He had grown fond of Ernie during the time they'd negotiated a contract, and now, hang the cost, Art was going to do everything possible to make Ernie's last months as pleasant as possible.

He had Ernie flown to Cleveland where he could undergo further examination and be among friends. Ernie arrived at Marymount Hospital the day of the All-Star game, and John Brown, John Wooten, and I drove in from Hiram to sit with him and watch the game that night on TV.

Not once did Ernie speak of his disappointment in being out of the game. He told us about various players on the All-Star squad–how big they were, how talented. He was touched when it was announced that the Packers had voted to award him the game ball.

Soon Ernie's doctors permitted him to vist our training camp, but he had to return to the hospital each evening. We often asked ourselves: "Does he know how sick he really is?"

We received an answer a few weeks later. Ernie was sent to Bethesda, Maryland, for a checkup. When he returned to Cleveland Modell and DeFilippo picked him up at the airport. Later they found on the back seat of the car, where Ernie had been sitting, a booklet of burial services. It had slipped out of his pocket.

In Cleveland, Dr. Victor Ippolito, the Browns' team physician, called in Dr. Austin Weisberger, one of the nation's foremost hematologists, to take over Ernie's case. As it was with everyone who got to know Ernie, a close friendship developed between the two.

No longer confined to the hospital, Ernie took an apartment with John Brown–he called him Johnbrown–and attended our exhibition games. And suddenly, a development occurred that Dr. Weisberger described as "semi-miraculous."

Ernie entered a state of complete remission, meaning tests showed his blood count normal in all respects. Dr. Weisberger explained that it's not uncommon for adults to become partly remissive, but the total remission that Ernie experienced was remarkable. One could scarcely guess, however, how long it would last.

Dr. Weisberger and Art Modell agreed, at any rate, that it was time to tell Ernie he had leukemia. Already there was too much whispering. John Brown had told us that Ernie had gone to a movie and been approached by a stranger, who asked him, "Are you Ernie Davis?"

"No," said Ernie. He never liked people to fuss over him; adulation made him uncomfortable.

"You're lucky," the stranger said. "Ernie Davis has leukemia and he's going to die in six months."

"I'm Ernie Davis," Ernie replied quietly, "and I'm not going to die."

Later, Ernie explained to John Brown, "I didn't want to hurt that man but it might keep him from being cruel to somebody else."

Dr. Weisberger broke the news to Ernie gently. Later, the doctor and Art Modell described the meeting to me. Dr. Weisberger had cushioned the blow by quickly telling Ernie his remission was so complete that he could now play football. This news brightened him considerably but it didn't eliminate the fact that he finally knew he had cancer of the blood. The first thing he said was, "Can I lick it?" Dr. Weisberger replied that leukemia victims have been known to live normal lives for a long time. Ernie perspired a little but remained silent. The doctor said, "You're an intelligent person, Ernie. You must have had some inkling."

"Yes. I thought about the possibility," Ernie said. "But I made myself stop thinking about it. I made up my mind that whatever I had I was going to have to live with it and make the most of it."

Dr. Weisberger told me, "I don't believe for a minute that he wasn't upset, but he never showed it. Not once."

Ernie asked only that his illness be kept a secret, but when he was told that his ability to play football would provide a lift for other leukemia patients he agreed to a carefully worded statement to be issued to the press.

As matters turned out, Ernie's role with the Browns never went beyond doing calisthenics with the squad and running laps around the field while we practiced plays. Running those laps, he must have known a terrible loneliness. But the uniform he now wore gave him hope, and he kept running.

Actually, none of us really expected Ernie to play football. Joining the squad late, he was simply too far behind in conditioning and timing and indoctrination. We had been working together for weeks, and it was too late for Paul Brown to put a new man—a rookie—into the lineup. Even had Paul put Ernie on the active roster, he would have had to bump off a more seasoned, conditioned player. Ernie knew this, yet at the same time he had a right to dream of a miracle. At times I wished that Paul would tell Ernie to run a few plays with us, but I imagine Paul was afraid of building Ernie's hopes too high.

Meanwhile, if there had been any doubt in my mind that Ernie had the makings of a great pro, I had no such doubt now. He had proved in college that he had the necessary size and speed. Now, by his very behavior, he was proving that he had the necessary courage and class. But what of his head? Did he have the football mind that separates the men from the boys?

There is no question he did. For a rookie, his grasp of football was amazing. Most players think in terms of their own positions, paying little attention to others, but Ernie Davis thought total football. In a mere matter of days and weeks, and merely from watching from the sidelines, he made observations that were beyond many veterans. For example, during a lull in practice one day he fell to discussing Bernie Parrish, one of our defensive backs.

Bernie was, and is, highly regarded throughout the league. He has covered the league's best flankers one-on-one—such flankers as Tommy McDonald, Buddy Dial, Red Phillips, Sonny Randall. These are lightning-quick men. Consequently, most players in the league—even Bernie Parrish's teammates—assume that Bernie himself is speedy. But Ernie Davis, after taking only a few brief looks at him, told me: "That Parrish must really be a student of the game. He's not very fast and he's not even very quick. But he seems to know just where to be. He must have a tremendous knowledge of opposing players, don't you think? He seems to know their likes and dislikes and what they'll do in certain circumstances. He's my idea of an amazing ballplayer."

I was startled by Ernie's analysis of Parrish. Bernie had been a high school sprinter, and yet it was true—by N.F.L. standards, he was not fast. I had held exactly the same view of him that Ernie expressed, but I had put in four years playing with Parrish. Ernie had analyzed him almost at a glance.

Similarly, he was quick to see that Vince Costello, our middle linebacker, was among the best in the league, even though Vince had gone unrecognized. He is small—only six feet tall—and thus does not seem fierce. As middle linebackers go, Vince isn't fast. But Ernie saw Vince's value almost immediately.

"That guy hardly ever makes a mistake, does he?" Ernie said to me. "He's a sure tackler, and on pass defense he seems to fall into his area beautifully."

Those were my thoughts exactly, and again I was impressed to hear them from a rookie. I do not say this patronizingly, but rather out of thorough admiration for Ernie's ability to grasp that which had taken me years.

Ernie watched us play the New York Giants and later spoke to me about a Giant defensive star who had a big name and was feared throughout the league. Most young players took it for granted he couldn't be moved.

"Jim, it seems to me that he comes wide," Ernie told me. "He doesn't really come in hard against the run. He looks like an easy shot to run right at." Again, Ernie was right. I never expressed my opinions of players to Ernie until I had heard his. It was more fun waiting to hear him hit the nail on the head.

Ernie's interest in football was consuming, yet he had to stand on the edge of the practice field and be content to watch. When Paul Brown left in January and many of us publicly stated that we were glad, Ernie only said, "From the little I know of Paul Brown, I think he is a fine gentleman." Ernie always meant what he said. In private conversations with me, he always spoke respectfully of Paul.

The football season had come and gone, and Ernie had us telling ourselves that he would make it—that his semi-miraculous complete remission might last. He was strong. He had run longer and harder than the rest of us in practice. He had bowled and played golf with us and held his own. At no time did he so much as allude to his leukemia. And now, with winter coming on, he joined the Cleveland Browns basketball team. He played like a tiger.

But in February Ernie began to slip out of his remissive state and was advised by Dr. Weisberger to stop playing basketball "for a while." The doctor told him he needed further blood therapy—medication and transfusions. All Ernie said was "Darn."

"That," Dr. Weisberger told me, "was the only complaint, literally and truly, that Ernie ever made in all the times I saw him." In point of fact, Ernie's refusal to complain made it impossible for Dr. Weisberger to question him about symptoms. Blood tests had to be made to evaluate his condition. He always told the doctor: "I feel fine. I feel strong." He didn't want to be a bother to anyone.

When Ernie needed transfusions he refused to stay overnight in the hospital. He wanted none of us to know he was slipping. Only once did he speak of his illness. John Brown told me:

"We were sitting in the apartment one night, and I was talking about marriage, life, the hard road you have to travel, the things that sometimes make you afraid to take a step. Ernie listened to me and then he said, 'I may not make it, John. But that doesn't mean I have to quit trying.' "

Each night Ernie shut the door to his room for a few moments of privacy, probably for prayer.

I saw a good deal of Ernie during the last winter of his lifetime. We bowled together and went to parties together. We shopped together, indulging our mutual weakness for clothes.

Ernie loved tasteful clothes. He favored the Eastern cut and the old English cut and the Ivy League cut (though not the commercial Ivy style). Together, we bought Italian car coats, and Ernie also had himself fitted for a British walker. Each garment added to his wardrobe announced that Ernie had no intention of giving up.

In his quiet way, he was fiercely determined that no one should see him as a sick man. He talked about next season, when he would be playing for the Browns. He went around to Art Modell's office looking for work to keep him busy, and Art assigned him to study game films and draw up analyses of opponents.

"He made a helluva study," assistant coach Dick Evans told me. "He put down every move. It's really fantastic."

But Ernie continued to slip. We planned to go to a party together one night, so I stopped by his apartment to pick him up. He looked terribly tired. I wanted to say, "Look, Ernie, if you're a little tired or if you feel a little under the weather, why not skip the party?" I wanted to back out of the party, but I knew if I did Ernie would know why. If I had so much as mentioned that he looked tired, it would have been like hitting him in the belly.

We sat there and talked a while, and all the time I hoped he'd say, "I'm a little bushed tonight, Jim. I think I'll skip the party." But of course, he didn't say anything of the kind. While we talked I noticed, suddenly, that Ernie had a small wad of cotton stuffed into his nose. He had stuffed it well up where it could not be easily seen, but it slipped down. Ernie's hand leaped to his face. He pretended to be idly fingering his nose while he stuffed the cotton back into place. I looked the other way, pretending not to notice. I was sick at heart. Nosebleeds, I knew, were a grave sign. That speck of cotton told me it was the beginning of the end.

We went to the party, which actually was a quiet gathering

of friends. Others noticed the cotton, but everyone played Ernie's game. They pretended they hadn't seen.

Soon after, I saw Ernie at another party, four or five days before he died. I got there late and had gone only because I knew Ernie was there. (Lately, his neck had begun to swell and he was in great pain, but all he said was that he might be having some tooth trouble.) There weren't many people at the party. Mostly, those who were there were playing cards. "It's not very lively here," Ernie said to me, as if to say he preferred a livelier time. "I think I'll go home." That was the last time I saw Ernie alive.

Two days before he died he had an appointment with Dr. Weisberger. John Brown woke him up to remind him of the appointment, and then left for work. Before going to the doctor, Ernie stopped by Art Modell's office to visit. "This was strange," Modell told me later. "He usually phoned first. Now I realize he was coming in to say goodbye."

When John Brown returned home that night he found a note from Ernie:

"Have to go to the hospital for a few days. Don't tell anybody. I'll see you around."

And so Ernie died the way he wanted to, inconveniencing nobody. I know of no greater humility. Ernie Davis was not afraid to die. But he was embarrassed for grieving his friends.

The city of Elmira stopped to say a silent goodbye to Ernie. The people overflowed the First Baptist Church. Outside, they stood shoulder to shoulder in the crisp early-spring of May. They lined the road to Woodlawn Cemetery–folks who had known Ernie Davis, boy and man. His power and grace, so perfectly interwoven as to suggest art, had delighted their eyes, and his gentle nature had warmed their hearts. At twenty-three, he was gone.

Our four-engine chartered plane, carrying Cleveland players, coaches, and front-office executives, hummed toward Cleveland.

Nobody talked. Ernie had been buried, but his death was still almost impossible to believe. I thought about words–such words as "great" and "courage." In the hullaballoo of sports, they are overused and abused. But I knew that Ernie Davis was the greatest, most courageous man I had ever met.

He will be remembered. In Elmira, the junior high school he attended has been named after him. The All-American Football Game, held each summer in Buffalo, established a memorial trophy to be given in his name to "the player who most impressed his coaches with a general attitude of cooperation, leadership, cheerfulness, and all-around conduct on and off the field."

An Ernie Davis Leukemia Fund, affiliated with the American Cancer Society, has been created by the Cleveland Browns. Art Modell, who had broken down and cried at the news of Ernie's death, started the fund with a sizable contribution. Art keeps a large photo of Ernie above his desk. "When I need a little extra lift I think of him," Art told me.

When I myself think of Ernie, I often remember him by an order of custom-made shirts that at the time of his death were still being cut at Larry Simon's in Cleveland. He had ordered the shirts only days before he died. To the end he remained determined to live as a man with a future. Without show, without an ounce of self-pity, he refused to quit in his corner.

The small boy writing to Dr. Weisberger said it best:

"He was so nice. . . . I loved him. . . . I'll never forget him."

PART III

OBSERVATIONS

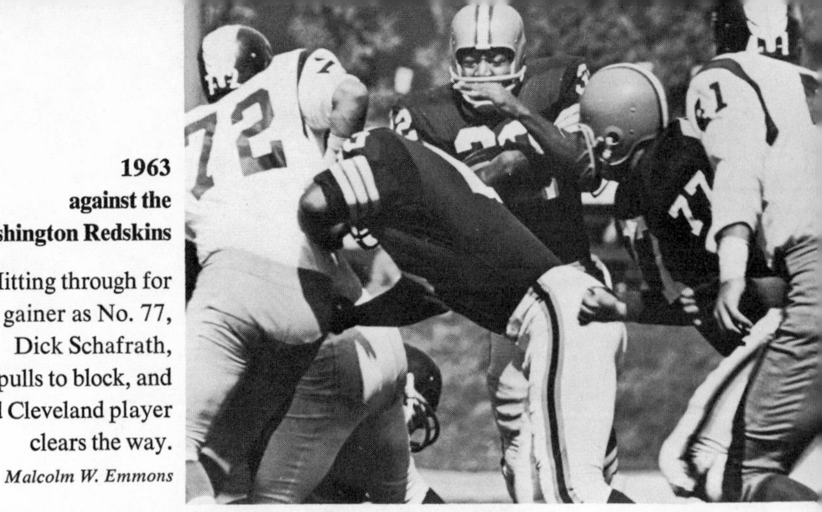

1963
against the
Washington Redskins

Hitting through for short gainer as No. 77, Dick Schafrath, pulls to block, and unidentified Cleveland player clears the way.

Malcolm W. Emmons

5

1963
against the
Washington Redskins

Deciding whether or not to go straight ahead or to cut behind John Brewer, No. 83.

1963
against the
Washington Redskins

Quarterback Frank Ryan smiles as No. 71 of the Redskins is about to get stiff-armed. Play resulted in first down.

Malcolm W. Emmons

1963 against the Philadelphia Eagles

Frank Aleksandrowicz

Breaking away for long touchdown run as Ben Scotti (on the ground) and Don Burroughs, No. 45, miss tackle.

Turning on speed. *Malcolm W. Emmons*

Frank Aleksandrowicz

CHAPTER 1

The free, white, and twenty-one Negro

Among Negroes in pro football today, there is one cardinal rule that each of us expects the other to follow: "Assert your dignity."

When a Negro rookie reports to a club he soon learns what sort of conduct the Negro veterans expect of him. (This is certainly true in the Cleveland organization, and I assume it is so in the others.) No committee of elder statesmen awaits the rookie with a lecture, but in a gradual fashion—or as the Supreme Court would say, with all deliberate speed—we try to instill bearing in him.

"Don't try to clown to win friendship," I've told young players. "Don't seek false friendship by being something a white man wants you to be. Generally, he expects you to be a jolly fellow, always laughing. When he wants to talk foolishness he comes to you, but when he wants to talk seriously he goes to a white man. Realize this attitude and cut it off from the beginning. Let the white man know you're interested in the same things he is—getting ahead, having a nice life, a home, a family, and so forth. Then if he accepts you on that basis, you're at least headed in the right direction."

If the rookie has just come from one of the small Negro colleges–say, Grambling or Florida A&M–and feels indebted to the coach who signed him out of obscurity, we tell him to smarten up. "This ball club," he is told, "is a business organization. The people who run it need you to do a job. That's why they brought you here. So don't go around acting like they did you a tremendous favor."

We are not trying to make the rookie hostile, nor are we trying to squelch his sense of humor. But we are determined to make him aware so he'll be able to detect the difference between a white teammate who wants him to dance and flash his white teeth and a white teammate whose friendship is genuine. We are not bossy about this, nor do we want the rookie to be constantly probing and evaluating his white teammates. His own good sense will tell him that Jim Shofner, for example, is his teammate in every sense of the word. Shofner is a defensive halfback who comes from Texas. He is just a good, good man who could never conceive of treating a teammate like a freak. He gives respect and gets respect. You don't probe a Jim Shofner; you don't wonder about his politics. Jim and I don't socialize together off the field, but I don't have to socialize with him to know he is an honest man with great character.

On the other hand, I wouldn't enjoy seeing a Negro rookie laughing for the entertainment of a teammate like the one who used to say to us Negro players:

"Where'd you guys go last night? You guys meet any good babes last night?"

"What do you mean, 'you guys'?" I finally asked him. "Who do you mean by 'you guys'?"

Obviously he regarded the six or seven Negroes on the squad as an inseparable nightlife safari. I socialize with football players and non-football players, with Negroes and whites. Negro football players do not, as our teammate seemed to assume, eat together, sleep together, and go to the bathroom together. So I saw to it that I was never asked about "you guys" again.

Long ago, the Negro proved he could compete with the white man on the field, but he continues to be reminded that he is part of a breed that is not quite as bright as his white colleagues. You are reminded when you hear a coach brief you on such proven defensive stars as Jimmy Hill of St. Louis and Night Train Lane of Detroit. "That fellow," the briefing goes, "has great *inborn* ability." And then, with index finger thumping against the temple, "But he *can't think.*"

I have no bones, no muscles that the white man doesn't have; I have no resiliency or speed handed down from my jungle heritage. But I do have as much dignity as any white man, and if this is not recognized in Mississippi I at least expect it to be recognized by my teammates and employers. In 1960 Paul Brown came to me and asked why all of our Negro players hung together when appearing at football luncheons and banquets. "All the Negro players sit in a group apart from our white players," said Paul. "People are commenting about this. It doesn't help us look like a team."

I replied that we were not going to make a show of looking chummy as long as the club's business manager assigned us hotel rooms in a manner that suggested we had leprosy. We had no objection to the fact that Negro players invariably were roomed with Negro players, and whites with whites. On one recent trip, however, our squad had consisted of an odd number of Negroes and an odd number of whites. Instead of pairing off the extra Negro with the extra white, the business manager had given them separate rooms. In other words, he was willing to pay for an additional room in order to preserve the color line. Jim Marshall, the Negro who had been given a private room, did not strike me as a person who would contaminate a white man. I told Paul Brown the setup smacked of small thinking. He said he was unaware of it, and would correct it. Thereafter, we mixed with white players at banquets.

Looking back on the seven years I have spent in pro football, it is perhaps surprising that I can recall only two instances when opposing players hurled racial slurs at me. In my rookie year a Detroit Lions defensive back called me a "black sonofabitch." I in turn shot him a cool look which told him I did not intend to lower myself to his level by replying.

The second incident was more amusing than offensive. The week before the 1963 season opened, we played an exhibition game against the Pittsburgh Steelers in Canton, Ohio. On a third-down play, a defensive lineman objected to the way I landed on him. I told him, "Go run up a tree," or somewhat saltier words to that effect. I then turned to trot off the field to make way for the punting team. As I left I heard the lineman call after me:

"Why don't you go back to the Mafia where you came from?"

I stopped in my tracks, puzzled. I turned back and said:

"Back to the *Mafia?* Hey, fella, you better take a good look at me. I've never passed for Italian before."

I sort of felt sorry for this bright fellow because he was standing there fuming and stuttering and groping for something to say. So out of frustration he spoke the obvious: "Why don't you go back with the rest of the niggers?" I trotted off the field, relieved that I was back in the good graces of the Justice Department.

The fact that I have so seldom been a target for slurs on the field neither pleases nor displeases me. It is a matter of little consequence. I do not crave the white man's approval; I crave only the rights I'm entitled to as a human being. The acceptance of the Negro in sports is really an insignificant development that warms the heart of the Negro less than it does that of the white man, who salves his troubled conscience by telling himself, "Isn't it wonderful that Negroes and whites are out there playing together?"

The problem is a little bigger than a ball game.

Consequently, I have no desire to discuss "the role of the Negro in sports," or some such nicely limited topic. I will speak of the problems and feelings of the Negro athlete because I am, after all, a Negro athlete, but I shall go beyond sports into areas where some may challenge my competence. My views–strong views–are not original, yet I am in a better position than most Negroes to attempt to awaken the white man to the fact that the time is not tomorrow but now. I'm one of those niggers who "ought to be glad to be here." I make big money. I enjoy fame and even adulation. My future is assured. Nevertheless, I am not thankful to be here. If anything, I am more angry than the Negro who can't find work.

So far as the presence of the colored man in professional sports is concerned, I can find only one small note of social advancement. Southern whites coming into pro ball are, for the first time in their lives, exposed at close quarters to the black man. There is a difference between knowing all the field hands by their first names and being forced to work and travel with black teammates. The Negro football player is not good old Mose who sweeps out the general store; he is college-educated, well paid, and proud. To borrow a slightly ill-fitting phrase, he is free, white, and twenty-one. So for the white southerner who becomes his teammate, an educational process begins.

This process is to the good, but even so, I doubt it accomplishes much. White teammates, whether southern or otherwise, may develop respect and even affection for a colored player, but there is a tendency to think of him as an exception to the rule. In other words, he's not one of those shiftless Negroes.

The old stereotypes persist. I recall a time when the Browns were training in Forest Grove, Oregon, for an upcoming exhibition game in Portland. One night John Wooten and I fell to discussing the Negro rebellion with a white teammate, a man with whom I disagree but whom I admire because he has the guts to sit down with us and frankly criticize the American Negro. "The Negroes," he told us that night, "have contributed a lot to sports and entertainment but it would be a lot better if they contributed in other fields. If they want to be accepted as equals, they'll have to do more than play ball and be good musicians."

"Do you realize," I asked him, "that there might be Negroes contributing importantly in other fields whom you're not aware of?"

"Like who?"

"Well, like Ralph Bunche."

"Ralph Bunche? Who's Ralph Bunche?"

I was stunned. If he didn't know who Ralph Bunche was, he was so uninformed that there was no point in continuing the conversation. I arose and said, "It's getting late. I'm going to my room." John Wooten stayed behind to continue the conversation but our white teammate realized that I thought it ridiculous that he had never heard of Ralph Bunche. When the team returned to Cleveland he asked his wife to go to the public library and get him a few books on the American Negro. He made a conscious effort to know more about us, and subsequently we had excellent discussions, though we continued to disagree.

I puzzled him. "Look, Jim," he would say, "you have a lot of things to be thankful for. You have a good salary and millions of kids think you're great. You ought to be happy." There, in a nutshell, is the great fallacy that boils my blood. It is a contradiction to end all contradictions.

In the first place, I needn't thank my lucky stars for being successful, because I worked hard to achieve success. Through grade school, high school, and college, I was taught democracy. Teachers taught me the same things they taught the white kids sitting next to me. I was taught that America is the land of free enterprise, the land of the individual; that every man can have a chance to be President; that if a kid worked hard and went to college and got educated, he would have a chance to make a decent living. I was taught the *American* culture, not a foreign culture. I was taught that our country is set up to give a man a chance to go as far as his ability and ambition and energy will take him. So today I cannot say to myself, "Considering your ancestors were slaves, you're lucky to be where you are."

The fact is, the more successful a Negro is, the more difficult it becomes for him to accept second-class citizenship. Can anyone possibly think that it does my heart good to sign twenty autographs in a hotel lobby and then be turned out of the hotel dining room? All right, I'm a big football star so a white man living in, say, Texas invites me to his home, knowing his neighbors may disapprove. I can sense beyond a doubt that he thinks he is making a big, bold, defiant move. It galls me. No matter how much money I make or how many yards I gain or how well I conduct myself as an American citizen, it is still a feat of courage for that man to take me home to dinner.

I doubt that the American white man realizes that the time has come when he must make a move. He must give us the laws that make us free men, and he must enforce those laws. If he thinks this can be achieved gradually, he knows nothing of the modern Negro–the Negro of my generation. I am not interested in winning freedom for my three children. Both my wife Sue and I have gone through college learning the principles of democracy, and we intend to have democracy while we're young enough to enjoy it. "Go forth and live in heaven," we are told. "Die and then you will live." But the white man lives today. I, too, intend to live today. If I make heaven, that's a bonus. I hope we can win freedom peaceably, but I'm skeptical. Great battles for freedom have seldom been won peaceably.

The most discouraging fact of all is that the American white man simply does not understand the black man. Perhaps I should qualify that by saying very few white men understand us. Most whites do not realize that we have been suppressed so long that we have developed new faculties of sight and hearing, that in the company of whites we can fairly see and hear their minds working. The eyes and ears grow sharp. In the presence of whites we need no more than a single word or a fleeting facial expression to communicate an entire thought to one another.

Few whites realize that we have even developed a language—not really a language but an idiom—of our own. A white man is a "fay." A Negro is a "member." A car is a "short." A party is a "set." The Negro's idiom is not meant to be derogatory to the white man; it's merely slang, and like most slang it serves to make conversation lighthearted and more fun. But when necessary it can come in handy—a single word can be spoken to alert a fellow Negro to a situation, with the white man none the wiser.

The white's ignorance of the Negro is understandable. The white man is on top. He knows he has more government and more resources and more opportunity than the black man, and consequently he is not going to worry deeply about the desire that thrives in the black man's heart. Human nature, I suppose. But today the Negro is aware of government and resources and opportunity, and his mood is explosive. So the white man had better start trying to understand him.

The first thing the white man must understand is the depth of our protest. Does he realize that the Black Muslims' basic attitude toward whites is shared by almost 99 percent of the Negro population? I protest prejudice, but I am a prejudiced man. The white man has forced me to be prejudiced against *him.* I do not hate. Hate is stupid; it allows no room for reason. When I look at my white teammates I see pleasing traits and displeasing traits, just as they may find me both pleasing and displeasing. When you are exposed to a man you cannot hate him unless you are sick. Yet I am *prejudiced,* which is not the same state of mind as hate. I am skeptical of white men because even the best of them want me to be patient, to follow Martin Luther King's advice and turn the other cheek until God knows when.

I am not a Black Muslim, but rather a member of the more rational NAACP, and yet I'm all for the Black Muslims. We need every possible element going for us, whether it be a radical sect, a CORE picket line, or a team of NAACP lawyers arguing in court. The more commotion the better. Yet it is indicative of the white man's ignorance of our attitudes that when you ask whites —intelligent whites—what sort of organization they think the Muslims are, they almost invariably answer something like this: "The Muslims are extremists. They're the counterpart of the Ku Klux Klan."

The fact is, they are not. They don't stalk into the night and burn crosses and terrorize people and flog them. They hurt nobody. On the contrary, they preach against drinking, against smoking, against adultery. Not unlike the Pennsylvania Dutch sects, their women wear long dresses. The Muslims preach neatness, cleanliness, and courtesy. Where is the parallel between them and the Ku Klux Klan?

Certainly if a Muslim approaches the average Negro in the street and tells him every white man is a devil and that we Negroes must one day form a separate nation, the Negro in the street will laugh at him. Such notions are stupid. But most of what the Muslim says about the white man is not one iota different from the conversation I hear among all Negroes, from the lowest economic class to the business and professional level.

Do I sound bitter? I am not in the least bitter. You don't have to be bitter to fight. If people throw rocks at your home, you don't have to be bitter to come out ready for action.

Speaking for myself, I do not want the white man's love. If he will love me, fine, but I ask only for just laws and the enforcement of them. I heard Martin Luther King say, "Smite me on my left cheek and I shall turn my right, and I shall still love you." Personally, I cannot believe that freedom will be won through love. I cannot love a man who clouts me. Dr. King is a great man because he has courage and because he has the ability to draw the masses together and move them and therefore make a tremendous contribution to the Negro restlessness, but he is a preacher, a speechmaker. I for one will not march down the street and kneel and pray for my rights. That is just not my shot. I prefer the dispassionate approach of such spokesmen as James Farmer of CORE and A. Philip Randolph of the Brotherhood of Sleeping Car Porters, men who deal in facts and figures that prove the Negro is discriminated against by employers and by unions and by government. But the white man again fails to understand us if he leaps to the conclusion that we are a house divided and will fall; all of us are protesting in our own way, and we know that if peaceful means fail, the black man, whether Muslim or whatever, will be on the side of the black man.

Shallow minds may argue that my position is a contradiction. How, on the one hand, can I acknowledge that I have known and loved white men who educated me and furthered my career but on the other hand cheer the Muslims, who claim all white men are devils? Have I forgotten that the great majority of Cleveland football fans–fans who have treated me with immense warmth –are white?

I see no contradiction. The issue is much larger than my own relationships with white friends and fans. I give each individual the respect that he gives me, but the white race as a whole has its heel on the Negro and that is what this whole thing is about.

When I say I am not bitter I say further that I am not even angry. I can't walk around in a state of anger, boiling at the white race. If anger is involved here, it's the white man who's angry–he's angry at me for wanting a bigger piece of life. I meet this anger by being aware that I can't lie down quietly and take the easy way out.

Frequently I am invited by white friends to golf at their country clubs. I know their clubs bar Negroes from membership, yet I go. I go because I like to golf and enjoy the company of the man who has invited me. I do not object to the fact that his club is exclusive, nor to the fact that he belongs to it. This does not rankle me because I do not expect my white friends to join my fight to the extent of losing their own identity. I do not expect them to alienate their friends and associates by mounting a soapbox in my defense every time someone uses the word nigger. Let the whites keep their identity, but let them open every public, tax-supported golf course in America to Negroes.

I don't ask integration. I just don't want to be segregated. I have no urge to live in a white neighborhood, but if the house that best suits my fancy happens to lie in a white neighborhood I want that house. Shortly after I moved to Cleveland I went apartment-hunting. I wanted a comfortable apartment that would be convenient to our practice field and be situated in a neighborhood free of the hoodlum element. I was unable to rent. "We only take whites," I was told by the landlady of the building that I had picked out. "The hell with it," I told her. My great-grandmother had reared me to respect my elders and be courteous to women. I tip my hat. I do not even know the first name of the woman who for several years has done housework for my wife, simply because she is an elderly woman and I have always respectfully called her Mrs. Graham. I wouldn't think of calling her by her first name. But I had to tell that landlady, "The hell with it."

Though I did not want to buy, I ended up buying a house. I found a modest little house on a modest street that is almost entirely Negro. Doc Hines, the Negro physician who lives next door, can afford a much bigger place, just as I can, but we like our street. Our neighbors are responsible. Their children are well bred. Our wives can walk the streets at night without fear of hoodlums, white or Negro. These are the things we look for. We do not search for a place that has white neighbors, nor do we seek a place populated by Negroes. But if some day we want a bigger house, a nicer house, and it lies in an all-white neighborhood, we want the right to buy it. So again I say, the hell with integration–just don't segregate me.

When I ask the white man to understand me I ask him to

understand that I am an American, not an African. While I was in high school Jackie Robinson was a baseball star. People told him, "Jackie, you're a credit to your race." They meant this as a great compliment, yet Jackie was thinking that he was an American, that baseball was an American way of life, and that he ought to be regarded as a credit to America. The people who praised him meant well, but they sort of missed the boat. The Negro takes no pride in being a Negro, per se. How can biology command pride? Yet the Negro who wants to be proud of America is puzzled by the fact that after Americans have gone to war with Germans and Japanese they once again become friendly and respectful to Germans and Japanese while continuing to hate Negro Americans.

The very word Negro offends my ears. As a matter of convenience I use it to describe myself, but it has an almost foreign sound. Exactly what is a Negro anyhow? I have a friend who is called a Negro, but is he one? He has a fair complexion and straight hair. His ancestry is probably nine-tenths white. So if you must give him a race label, wouldn't you have to call him a white man? Unquestionably he could pass for white if he cared to. But then he might spend five years building a place for himself in the white community only to have someone discover one day that he has Negro blood. Overnight he would become an outcast. In a grim way this is funny. It tickles me to think of all the Negroes who have relatives on the White Citizens Councils and in the Ku Klux Klan.

Who knows? We might even have one or two Negroes who have passed over in pro football and are massaging their scalps while telling television audiences to throw away "that greasy kid-stuff." Which brings me to the matter of product endorsements.

Obviously, colored athletes receive a disproportionately small share of the endorsement dollar. I can readily understand that many advertisers would rather have Sam Huff speak for their product than, say, Jim Brown or Bobby Mitchell. If the market analysis shows that the use of a Negro on TV or on billboards would alienate a mass market in the white South, all right. That's business. Companies must compete to survive.

But it seems to me that advertisers are in many cases behind the times. For example, we know that many ad campaigns are aimed at children. ("Tell your mother you just love those golden Glumphies topped with a heap o' strawberries!") Now I know from my experience as an athlete that children are the least bigoted group in America. At the risk of sounding immodest, I can also say that it is *my* autograph that is most in demand by the children of Cleveland. Consequently, if an ad campaign is being aimed at them, what sense does it make to restrict my billboard picture to Negro neighborhoods? The thinking adman should ask himself, "What image will Jim Brown project? Will he project the Negro image or the athlete image?" Too often, the admen coast along in a rut, thinking of Negro athletes only when they want to aim at the Negro market.

The product endorsement situation is, of course, just one more instance of the triumph of the stereotype over fact. Repeatedly, the Negro encounters the white man taking refuge in stereotypes. And then again, the Negro who wants only to be judged on his own merits encounters another kind of automatic white reflex—the sympathetic pat on the back when none is deserved. My mind races back to a New Year's Eve in Miami Beach.

The Browns were training down there for the annual Playoff Bowl game. Several other Negro players and I gathered in my hotel room to watch the telecast of the annual New Year's Eve Orange Bowl Parade, a lavishly colorful affair. Presently a Negro band marched into view on the TV screen. "Boy, look at that band step!" cried the TV announcer. "That certainly is a high-stepping outfit!" We laughed. That band was average, no different than the one that had just preceded it. But the parade was probably 90 percent white and now here came this Negro band and the announcer was going to bend over backwards to show that he was a fair guy. High-stepping? If he had been talking about the Florida A&M band, an outstanding Negro marching unit, he would have been right, but here he was shouting about a band that would never win a prize. In other words, he was trying to give us more credit than we were due, which is simply a form of unconscious phoniness that the Negro runs into time and again.

So you see, we hear and we see—we listen closely and watch closely. We know the white man's mind much better than he knows ours, because we have had a lot of practice trying to know. We are continually having to size up our situation. Our antennas are up.

In Miami Beach I was golfing in a foursome. At the fourteenth hole a young white man and an elderly white couple began following us. They didn't interrupt our game for autographs. They were even helpful, now and then spotting a ball for us. When I came off the eighteenth green the elderly gentleman approached me and said: "My son went to Cornell and I saw you play against Cornell in your sophomore year. I really enjoyed your performance."

"Did you really see the Cornell game?" I said. "That was the game when my career really got started."

"Oh, yes. That halfback got hurt and you got into the game and got off a long touchdown run. You know, I've followed your career and admired you because each step of the way you've improved. I know Ed Walsh, your old high school coach, and I respect you all the more because you're one of Ed Walsh's boys."

This man's words really meant a lot to me, because you see, he had the facts and he was sincere. The antenna catches sincerity, too. Frequently, I'm glad to say. But all too often it catches insincerity.

Here, for example, is Jim Brown surrounded by people wanting his autograph. He obliges. Everyone in the circle of fans has a friendly smile for him. But now, suddenly, there is this little white girl, perhaps seven or eight years old, whose father tells her to say hello to Jim Brown. Jim Brown bends over to say hello to her. She senses that Jim Brown, the center of all this attention, is a celebrity and, God bless her, she has a feeling of affection for him. She wants to reach up and put her arms around his neck and kiss him on the cheek. But Jim Brown has had the experience, thank you. He can see that hug and kiss coming. And he knows that after the little girl has kissed him he will look up and find that all the smiling adult faces have been replaced by frozen faces. So he quickly maneuvers out of the little girl's range; he *finesses* his way out. And his heart hurts, because at that moment he loves that little girl just as she loves him.

You see, that's the way it is. One minute people look at you with regard, but the next minute you're an animal that shouldn't be kissed on the cheek by a little girl. A Texan named Y. A. Tittle, who is the finest quarterback in pro ball, goes on the Ed Sullivan show and calls you the best football player he has seen in his time . . . and the first man to relay this great compliment to you is a TV viewer named Lyndon Johnson, who has invited you to the White House. Well, don't go popping the buttons off your vest, big shot, because a few miles away in Virginia white folks are closing public schools lest their kids have to sit in the same room with your kind.

So how can you tell yourself, "I'm glad to be here because I'm a star and I make big money and the public cheers me"? You have to wonder if the white man will ever begin to understand you.

CHAPTER 2

Big Daddy

In pro football a good many players indulge in a practice known in the trade as "psyching." Psyching an opponent usually takes the form of trying to con him with conversation. Maybe you try to taunt him into committing a foul, or maybe you try to intimidate him with tough talk and threats. Personally, I don't go in for verbal nickel psychology; I don't converse with opponents during a game. But there was one man in the National Football League I always tried to psyche. He was the late Gene (Big Daddy) Lipscomb.

Naturally, I did not taunt or try to intimidate Big Daddy. Only a fool or a man bent on suicide would have tried that. What I did was try to psyche him into a frame of mind that would not allow him to get mad at me. I won't say I was afraid of Big Daddy, but on the other hand, I was conscious of the damage Daddy was capable of performing on us mortal men.

Six-feet-six and 290 pounds, Daddy rose up in the middle of the enemy line like the Empire State Building with a mustache. He had the strength of an elephant and was so fast he frequently ran down backfield men from behind. He was the one man in the league who by himself could practically control a play. What gave me pause was the known fact that Daddy could stop a ball carrier in his tracks with a great bear-hug, then straighten him up like a board, and then bend him every way imaginable. There was nothing illegal or dirty about this sort of thing. But just thinking about it, you could feel your spine splintering. You knew it wouldn't take much to give Daddy an excuse for twisting you into a piece of abstract sculpture. For one thing, he was the supreme showman: His shirttail always hung loose so it could flap in the wind when he ran. Crowds tittered when Daddy considerately leaned over and helped us little 230-pounders to our feet after smashing us to the ground. But above all, Daddy had the sensitive soul of an artist.

He was great when he wanted to be great, and the one thing that inspired him most was the chance to make mincemeat out of a star. That's where I first came in—in 1959, my third year of pro ball. Daddy played for Baltimore then, and this was our first meeting with the Colts since I had come into the league. He announced to the press that he was going to get "that Cleveland cat."

As it happened, I had a five-touchdown day—one of the best days that I have ever had. This was largely due to the fact that a guard named Jim Ray Smith was putting blocks on Daddy. Jim Ray was, and still is, the best blocking guard in the league. He and I were giving it to Daddy good in the first half. Just as Jim Ray would hit him, I would run straight at him. The next time Jim Ray hit him, I would slide off a couple yards to the side of Daddy. And the next time I would hit right behind Jim Ray again. Daddy was having a bad time. I could tell by the look on his face that he wasn't enjoying it.

At halftime, as I was walking off the field, Daddy trundled up alongside me.

"Look, Jimmy," he said, frowning. "You were laughing at me out there. I don't like that."

Laughing at Daddy? Man, I'd been running for my life.

"Daddy, I didn't say a thing. What are you talking about?"

"You were making fun of me, boy," Daddy insisted. "I'm gonna get you in the second half. You look out, I'm gonna get you. I thought you were my friend."

With that, Daddy disappeared, stomping into the Colt dressing room.

Fortunately, Daddy was not quite able to get me in the second half. Bobby Mitchell kept him too busy. Mitchell, then our halfback, kept sweeping the ends, and with all his ducking and dodging he was making Daddy look bad. Daddy didn't like that at all. Whenever he managed to get to Mitchell he tried to run him up on the bench. He looked like he wanted to kill Mitchell. He sort of forgot about me.

After the game Daddy came up alongside me again and looked down at me and said, "You had a pretty good one today. After you're dressed, come into my dressing room and talk to me."

Obediently I paid my respects to Big Daddy before leaving the park that day, and even though I'd run well against him I made up my mind that I would never again let him get mad at me. So in future games I psyched him.

"Daddy, you're really looking good out here today," I'd say after he'd knocked me down.

"You think so?" said Daddy, craving reassurance. "Thank you, Jimmy."

"Keep up the good work," I'd say as he helped me to my feet.

Sometimes I'd say, "Gosh, Daddy, I really hope you make all-pro this year."

"I'm tryin', Jimmy. I'm tryin'."

I was careful not to overdo the conversation, but I always made a point of inquiring about Daddy's health, usually after the first time he had bashed me to the ground, and wishing him a successful campaign.

In the off-season of 1963, when Big Daddy Lipscomb suddenly died in Baltimore and the police theorized that he'd had an overdose of dope, all of us who knew him well were stunned. He and I had become good friends. If Daddy was using dope, he certainly was fooling every friend he had. If he did pick up the habit later, it had to be only shortly before his death. I am still puzzled by the mysterious circumstances surrounding his death.

One thing I am sure of is that Daddy's obituaries did not always give a true picture of him. For example, it was written that he wore red neckties so bright that they would fairly burn your eyes at ten feet, and that he wore alligator shoes that looked like the alligator was still living. Actually, Daddy was one of the neatest, most conservative dressers you would want to see, and at one time was even considered a square. Lenny Moore, his Baltimore teammate, used to josh him because he bought old men's shoes—the kind with high tops. They were of soft leather, because Daddy apparently had corns. When he emerged from his square phase, he dressed mostly in tasteful blue business suits. Though a huge man, he never looked sloppy.

Many people considered Daddy uncouth. I suspect this stemmed from the fact that if he didn't like you he would tell you in a loud voice to get out of his way and actually wipe you aside. He was afraid of nobody, but I never saw him in a fist fight. He had good common sense and knew instantly when someone was trying to be smart with him in a subtle way. And he had a great sense of indignation. When a Baltimore teammate once threw a party for the team and excluded the Negro players, Daddy expressed himself the best way he knew how—by marching into the party and turning the place inside-out.

I liked him because he was, while many other things, basically a gentle man, and I liked him because he was outspoken. He would tell his coach or anybody else where to go when convinced he was being wronged. But if he liked you, there was nothing he wouldn't do for you.

Shortly before his death I played with Big Daddy in the Pro Bowl at Los Angeles. He was a Pittsburgh Steeler then, so we were both on the East squad. Both of us had goals that day. I wanted to win the Most Valuable Player trophy, which is voted by the press to the best back on the field, and Daddy wanted to win the Lineman of the Day trophy. Each of us had special reasons for wanting the trophies.

In the previous year's Pro Bowl game I'd won the MVP trophy but circumstances had rubbed some of the shine off it. The press box had been polled minutes before the game ended. No sooner had the reporters voted me the award when I committed a fumble. The West recovered and scored a touchdown to win by one point. With trophy in hand, I was the Most Valuable Goat. Now I wanted to win the award legitimately, and for another reason. I had just come off my poorest season, gaining less than a thousand yards for the first time since I was a rookie. A sprained wrist that had bothered me throughout the season was completely healed now, and I felt I could re-establish myself with a good game. Daddy wanted a trophy because he had been neglected somewhat by the press the past year, even though an all-pro. He wanted to prove he was still huge, fierce, foreboding Big Daddy.

From the opening whistle he played a tremendous game. He swarmed over the passer. Two or three times he actually ran down speedy Dick Bass on end sweeps. "Boy, Daddy, you're really looking good," I told him. "Keep it up and you gotta get the trophy." "You think so?" Big Daddy would say, and then he would go out and smear the passer again. "How you think I'm looking?" he'd keep asking me anxiously. He would march up and down the sidelines, clearing his head with smelling salts–in other words, putting on a show for the press box. He let them know he was there in a way nobody else in football could. He was still Big Daddy.

We both won our trophies. Daddy held his to his chest like a kid with a new Christmas toy. "We showed 'em, huh, Jimmy?" he said.

Daddy left this world with a victory. If there is a heaven above, I think bighearted Big Daddy had to make it. And if he did, those angels up there better be playing it smart and psyching him like I did.

CHAPTER 3

Opponents I have known

In seven years of pro football I have met a lot of interesting people, usually at the bottom of a pileup. So I shall just touch on a few of the many players who have pleased my eye or tickled my funnybone or massaged my skull. Naturally, I have to start with Sam Huff. Who else?

Over the years Sam and I have been pictured as the N.F.L.'s version of Hatfield-McCoy. From his middle linebacker position in the New York Giant defense (he now plays for the Washington Redskins), Sam has treated me harshly, causing many persons to conclude that there's a feud being waged. Actually, there is not an ounce of bad blood between Sam and me, but the publicity given this imagined feud hasn't hurt either of us and has even given us a few lines for banquet audiences. For example, Sam tells 'em:

"I remember one game in particular. The first time Brown carried the ball he rammed into the middle of our line. I came up fast and stopped him hard for no gain. As the pile untangled I sneered at him and said, 'Brown, you stink.' He didn't say anything. He just got up slowly, as he always does, and walked back to the huddle.

"The second time he carried, the same thing happened. I dived into the hole and stopped him for no gain. I sneered harder and said louder, 'Brown, you stink.' Again he didn't say anything. He just walked back to the huddle.

"The third time he carried, you guessed it—he drove into the middle but nobody stopped him. He got a couple of key blocks, exploded past me and the secondary, and raced sixty-five yards for a touchdown. Trotting back to the Browns' bench, he turned to me and grinned. 'Hey, Huff,' he shouted. 'How do I smell from here?' "

Much as I hate to squelch Sam's banquet yarn, honesty compels me to say Sam has taken to creating fiction.

It is true, however, that Sam seems to make a special effort when playing against me, yet that's only natural. I am the back who gets the headlines. If I were a middle linebacker playing against a back who gets the ballyhoo, I would make a special effort just as Sam does. Then, too, the Giant coaches usually give Sam license to concentrate on me, so he is able to position himself against me and follow my every step and nail me time and again. He plays hard but not dirty. In one game a few years ago, however, I thought he got a little out of line. He twisted my head at the bottom of a pile.

"This is not like you, Huff," I said. "This is not your style."

To the best of my recollection, that was the only time I found Sam's play objectionable. Normally I wouldn't even tell an opponent he was overdoing it, but in Sam's case I figured he might appreciate my opinion. We have been slamming into each other since the days when I played for Syracuse and he played for West Virginia.

The fact is, Sam and I have a common bond: Jim Taylor, the Green Bay fullback. I gather Taylor doesn't care much for either of us.

Sport Magazine once reported:

"Taylor resents always being compared with Brown and is gradually developing a large-sized dislike for the Cleveland back whom, of course, he does not even know." Well, every man to his own dislikes, but the case of Taylor vs. Huff has unnecessarily caused Sam considerable anguish.

Most fans will recall that when Green Bay played New York in the 1962 championship game, Taylor and Huff had a good many collisions that produced bitter feelings. Later, Taylor was quoted as saying:

"Sam Huff is a great one for piling on. Sam likes being there on top of the pile. But I'm not saying Huff played dirty against me. I haven't seen our game movies. But somebody was in there twisting my head, and somebody was in there digging a shoulder and elbow into me."

And then there were these further quotes:

"I had a few words with Huff about it. I can't remember exactly what I said but I would have to say he was piling on and I wanted that to stop. I still hurt from that game, particularly my elbow, and on an out-of-bounds play I bit my tongue and ended up swallowing blood for the rest of the game. . . . I don't know where the blow came from. . . . I never heard so many people criticizing a player as Huff has been criticized. I'm sure all his critics aren't Green Bay Packer or Jim Taylor fans."

Shortly thereafter Taylor came down with hepatitis, an inflammation of the liver, and his fans somehow concluded that the pounding he'd taken from Sam had caused his illness. Sam received stacks of nasty letters, and he is still trying to live down a reputation for dirty play. At the time he was taking a lathering from the public, the newspapers called me for comment and I told them:

"Well, the officials didn't penalize Sam, did they? So either he played cleanly or the officials should be blamed for being blind."

Sure Sam hit Taylor when he was down or going down. But was that piling on? What's piling on when Taylor carries the ball? He's a rough-and-tumble ballplayer who squirms and crawls and consequently forces his opponents to make very sure he's been stopped. He taunts them, too, so what are they going to do, pat him on the fanny? I'm not criticizing Taylor's style—maybe it's what gives him his fire—but having played against Huff more times than Taylor has, I say Sam does not cross the thin line between hard and dirty play.

In the early stages of Sam's career I felt he was overrated. He was an excellent linebacker but his publicity tended to picture him as a superman. The Giant crowds took a liking to him and chanted, "Huff! Huff! Huff!" and Madison Avenue picked up the ball and flooded television with Sam Huff product testimonials. He made the cover of *Time,* and C.B.S. telecast a half-hour documentary entitled *The Violent World of Sam Huff*. But suddenly Sam's image changed. The Taylor affair was one reason; another was the envy aroused by the ton of money Sam was making from endorsements. It became fashionable among fans and players to snicker at Sam's violent world. So now Sam is *underrated.* In 1963 he had one of his best seasons.

Some say Detroit's Joe Schmidt and Chicago's Bill George are better linebackers than Sam, but I wouldn't know because they're in the Western Conference and I don't see them as often. I know only that of all the linebackers I've played against, Sam Huff is as tough and competent as any.

So far as Schmidt is concerned, I've seen enough of him to know that the one characteristic that distinguishes his performance is that he is *sure.* He latches onto you and that's it. You're down. His tackling is the most perfectly executed that I have seen. It amazes me that not once have I ever seen Joe Schmidt finish a play in a dirty position—not even accidentally. I have never seen his hands in a man's face. He is always in a good tackling position. When you see him slamming into a ball carrier he always has both of the ball carrier's legs wrapped up or he is meeting the ball carrier in midair and then carrying him back. Other linebackers may take a swing at your head and miss you and then you go for twenty yards, but you never get that kind of gift from Schmidt. He is a guy who puts his shoulder into you and tackles you and you're *tackled,* and that's the best way I can describe him.

I don't object to the non-Schmidt types—the guys who go for the ball carrier's head. It's part of the game. In this respect, however, defensive backs in particular leave lasting impressions on me because they pose the last obstacle between me and a salary-raising touchdown.

New York cornerback Erich Barnes is aggressive and spirited. We are good friends but I know that if one of the Giants slows me down in the secondary, Erich will charge in and jolt me with a forearm. (There is nothing illegal or dirty about this.) Many defensive backs go up with pass receivers timidly, but Erich goes up rough. He plays the ball hard. Put him down as one of the best cornerbacks in the league.

Jimmy Hill, the St. Louis cornerback, is one of the great cornerbacks in football. When I was still green I learned the hard way about Jimmy Hill. I would break through the line and then see him coming at me and expect him to try to tackle me, but he wouldn't tackle me—he would clout me in the head with his forearm. This happened three times before I realized Jimmy was never going to tackle me.

His forearm, of course, was as good as a tackle because the ball carrier has to go down. You have to ride with the forearm and *let* it knock you down. If you fight it you get a broken jaw. You look silly going down so easily, but at least your face is still in one piece. Call me a coward if you will, but I went down nicely three times for Jimmy Hill.

One day he and the Cardinals came to Cleveland, and I was ready for him. The first time I swung around end I saw him coming. Before he could hit with his forearm, I stiff-armed him. It was like a sucker punch, really—sort of a quick jab, but with a lot of force behind it. Jimmy Hill went flying. Twice more that day I nailed him exactly the same way. And from that day on, whenever Jimmy and I met, it was a simple question of who was quicker.

Actually, Jimmy is the man who convinced me that I have been right in refusing to argue with opponents when the action gets a little rough. I not only refuse to argue with them, but make a practice of reacting to every collision the same way. When a guy has hit me hard enough to rattle my bones I get up without saying anything and walk back to the huddle without expression. When he has hit me a little less hard, I do the same thing. That way, my opponent never knows if he is getting under my skin. After a while I may begin to get under his skin. I call this my Grizzly Bear Psychology. If you hauled off and hit a grizzly bear with your Sunday punch and the bear didn't move, what would you do next? You would run.

Every time Jimmy Hill knocked me down he would stand over me and talk tough.

"You come back this way," he'd say, "and you'll get some more of that."

I never replied. Finally, in 1961, Jimmy and I were cast together as teammates on the East's Pro Bowl squad and we had a chance to become friends. Our lockers were side by side in a corner of the dressing room where the management carefully segregated all the Negro players. "I don't understand you," Jimmy said to me.

"Why's that?" I asked.

"Well, there's been many a time when I've hit you with my forearm and I *knew* it was a good jolt and I *knew* you were supposed to lay there and at least be hurt a little bit. But you'd always get up and walk away. I have to admit that bothered me. I finally told myself, 'What's the use?' "

Of course, Jimmy *had* hurt me. But his words now were exactly what I wanted to hear, because they confirmed the old Grizzly Bear Psychology. Two years later, during the 1963 season, I made up my mind that henceforth, under certain rough circumstances, I would fight, and I promptly had the first fist fight of my career. But that's another matter I'll go into in a later chapter. Right now, the topic at hand is defensive backs who spoil my salary runs; Larry Wilson, one of Jimmy Hill's teammates, is another guy I wish would go away.

A few years ago ballplayers wondered why I raved about Wilson. He was just a kid out of Utah—a lanky, blond kid who had come low in the draft and received practically no recognition. But I felt he would soon be a star, for by actual count he had cost me four touchdowns.

Playing safety, he cut me down on breakaway runs four times. I had to be mighty impressed because each time he was in a one-on-one situation, which is a difficult predicament for a defensive back in the deep secondary. Some of them react timidly, but Larry Wilson showed me a lot of nerve, a lot of determination, and great tackling. Each of the four times he cut me down, I had figured I was going all the way. In 1963, Wilson's fourth year in the league, he made all-pro, and I was glad to see him get the recognition he deserved.

Yale Lary and Night Train Lane, over in Detroit, are another pair who make my life miserable. Lary drives me half-crazy. I have yet to outfox him in a one-on-one situation. Every time I think he's going to tackle me he throws a block on me, and every time I think he's going to throw the block he tackles me. "Well," the layman might say, "what difference does it make?" It makes a lot of difference.

When I figure a man's going to block-tackle me I get light on my feet so I can sidestep him or jump over him. When I think he is going to tackle me I lower my shoulder and get my forearm ready. I can't get light on my feet and lower the boom at the same time. I have to make a quick decision whether to be fancy or rough. But Yale Lary outguesses me every time. I lower my shoulder to meet the tackle and he knocks me flying with a block. The trouble with writing a book is that you have to admit to a guy like Lary that he is outsmarting you.

I don't think I've gotten past Lary's cohort, Night Train Lane, more than twice in my career. Train is a rough guy—a give-and-take guy. In the Pro Bowl one year I drove over right tackle and hit Train head-on and knocked him out of my way and went all the way for a touchdown.

"Hot damn," I said to myself. "You've finally got the Train licked." The next day I learned Train had been playing with appendicitis.

From where I stand (and often fall), defensive linemen differ from defensive backs only in the matter of sound effects. With the backs it's crack! crack!—with the linemen it's thump! thump! Two of them, Ernie Stautner and Gino Marchetti, played so many years that I began to think they carried a lifetime guarantee. To me, Stautner typifies that Gas House Gang over in Pittsburgh. He comes taped up like Frankenstein's monster and twice as mean.

God only knows how old Stautner is. He was in the war and then spent four years in college and since then he has played fifteen seasons of pro ball. Anyone wanting to know when he was born will have to go over to Bavaria and interview the fraulein who served as midwife. Ernie says his old man, Joe Stautner, is the toughest drinker in East Greenbush, N.Y., and now that the old gent is retired he keeps limber by felling trees. So I suppose Ernie's football style is a case of heredity. He is ferocious. Also, he is shockingly honest about his own trade.

"Defensive linemen," he says, "are nothing but damned hamburger. Offense is an art. What the hell is a defensive man?"

Well, the kind of defensive man that Ernie was, at his peak, can best be described by a scene I witnessed one year in Los Angeles. It happened a few days before the Pro Bowl game.

Baltimore's Jim Parker, a huge offensive lineman who has been Johnny Unitas's main line of protection, was having dinner when a coach came up to him and informed him that assignments had been switched and he would have to play opposite Stautner.

"Stautner!" screamed Parker. "Oh, God."

With that, Parker buried his head in his huge hands. I thought he was going to cry.

"He can't be all that tough," someone said, whereupon Parker looked up and replied:

"Listen, man, the last time I played against that animal he put his head into my belly and drove me into the backfield so hard that when I picked myself up and looked around there was a path chopped through that field like a farmer run a plough over it."

Like Stautner of Pittsburgh, Marchetti of Baltimore plays defensive end and over the past dozen years probably has worried a few offensive men right out of football. To my mind, Lenny Ford, my teammate in my rookie year, was the greatest defensive end I've ever seen, but Gino Marchetti is the closest thing to Ford I've seen. He almost worried John Brown, our young offensive tackle, out of the league.

In 1963, when John was a second-year man battling to stay on the payroll after a so-so rookie year, we had an exhibition game coming up with Baltimore. Our players told John:

"If you can do anything against Marchetti, you'll have it made."

A few days before the game we looked at films of a Baltimore game. John sat through the film in a cold sweat. Marchetti was up there on the screen eating up some little guy, whose name I can't recall. (I suppose that was the end of him.) Marchetti was putting such a whipping on him that John must have thought he was Superman. So John was kind of worried as game time approached.

As matters panned out, John emerged from the game in good health and continued employment–thanks to the fact that Blanton Collier had decided to shield our passer with double blocking protection, thus putting me in a position to lend John a hand with Marchetti. Even with the two of us working on him, he was murder. John was supposed to see that Marchetti did not get in from the outside and I was to see he didn't get in from the inside. Every so often John drifted a little too far inside and let Marchetti slip around him, but I was able to get over there and brush Marchetti past the quarterback.

"Thanks!" John would cry out. "My God, this guy's tough!"

John knew that he couldn't afford to let Marchetti get to our quarterback once, because that's all the coaches needed to see.

Marchetti was quick as light–so fast that in a normal one-on-one situation he could get by a tackle without the man so much as touching him. Moreover, he carried himself like a leader; he gives off an air of strength. Player gossip has it that when Weeb Ewbank coached the Colts he never made a trade without first weighing Marchetti's opinion.

Being a backfield man myself, I pay close attention to other backfield men, partly because of natural curiosity and partly on the chance I might learn something. Don Bosseler, the Washington Redskins fullback, probably doesn't know it, but I'm indebted to him for enabling me to score a lot of touchdowns and make a lot of first downs.

Bosseler entered the league the same year I did, and after a time I noticed that he was extremely successful in hurdling the enemy line in short-yardage situations. I myself wasn't, so I decided to study films of Redskin games and try to learn the secret of Bosseler's success. I looked at those films till I was groggy, and finally the answer hit me. It was simple.

When the quarterback handed Bosseler the ball, Bosseler kept his eye on the defensive linemen. If they submarined–that is, if they shot in low, trying to work under the Redskin line–Bosseler hurdled over them. When they did not submarine, he hit straight ahead. That was all there was to it.

In fact, Bosseler's method was so downright simple and logical that one would think it would be a standard fundamental taught by all football coaches when they are not running from clinic to clinic to enlarge on their technical know-how. Not so. A coach's instructions to fullbacks in short-yardage situations consist of saying:

"Hit hard in there, dammit! I want you to go in *voom!* Lower that shoulder!"

"Hit hard" is the favorite dictum of the coaching profession because it implies toughness, gameness, competitive spirit, and a willingness to work. I don't want to tell coaches their business, but when that defensive line submarines you can hit in there like a ten-ton truck and all you get is nothing.

Old John Henry Johnson of Pittsburgh is another fullback who knows how to hurdle a line. He is probably one of the most aggressive players in the league. He is tough and he blocks and runs quite hard.

Because I do not play defense and therefore do not come into contact with John Henry, I get a kick out of watching him play. Carrying the ball, he jumps all over the lot. He runs sideways, then swings back up the field, then hurdles clear over a tackler. He looks like a man having a running fit. But the best entertainment sometimes happens when John Henry hits smack into the center of the line.

Those defensive men stack in there to meet him like mad dogs, every one of them wanting a piece of him. So what happens, sometimes, is that you see John Henry charge head-first into that wild mess of beef, and the next second you see him running backwards right out of it. Watching this, I get the feeling I'm viewing a film that's being run back.

Although I've had no firsthand experience with Vince Lombardi, I admire him as much as any coach in the league. After Lombardi became head coach of the Green Bay Packers in 1959, more Packers suddenly became stars than seems possible.

Paul Hornung, Jim Taylor, Bart Starr, Ron Kramer, Willie Davis, Henry Jordan, and others—so many new stars it was just amazing. Jim Ringo (recently traded to Philadelphia) probably is the best center in football. A lot of centers can't "throw"—that is, they can't throw the lightning cross-body block that cuts down the defensive back trailing the play—but Ringo throws to the legs before a man can even begin to step out of his way. Yet Jim Ringo was, I believe, on the verge of retirement when Vince Lombardi came along.

Green Bay's two biggest names are, of course, my old pal Paul Hornung and Jim Taylor, who doesn't seem to want to be my pal.

Paul's forte is versatility. He runs, passes, blocks, receives, and kicks. Of those five talents, blocking is Paul's best. As a runner he is very good yet not the devastating type, but he is probably the best backfield blocker in the league.

As the girls well know, Paul also is probably the most attractive personality in football. After Commissioner Pete Rozelle suspended him for the 1963 season because he had bet on his own games, Paul made a nice buck touring the banquet circuit, and I finally met up with him again at a winter banquet in Erie, Pennsylvania. After the banquet I drove him to the airport.

"Making any money?" Paul inquired.

"Well, Paul," I replied, "I just had to give up a big one up in Regina, Canada. They were going to pay me seven hundred dollars and expenses for a banquet talk, but I've had to cancel out because I've got a job to do that day for Pepsi-Cola. I told them they ought to get in touch with you."

"Whooo-eeee," said Paul, rubbing his palms together. "Let's see. They were going to give you seven hundred, and now they don't have you, which means they're in a jam. I'll ask for a grand."

"A *thousand dollars?*" I exclaimed.

"Why not? I'm in a perfect spot."

Several days later I appeared at a banquet in Saskatoon, Canada, and was approached by a man who introduced himself as chairman of the Regina banquet. He carried a tape-recorder and wanted me to tape a short talk explaining to the Regina folks why I wouldn't be able to make their banquet. "By the way, I suppose you got Paul Hornung," I said to him.

"Oh, no," he replied. "That fellow wanted too much money. We got Jerry Kramer, the Green Bay guard."

I chuckled all the way back to Cleveland. Just imagine, a guard eating Paul's lunch!

Jim Taylor puzzles me. I don't understand his animosity toward me. I don't understand why he seems to feel that in order to secure his place as one of football's top fullbacks he has to knock me.

I told Paul Hornung at that banquet in Erie:

"Paul, I wish Taylor and I could sit down together just once and talk. I'd like to explain to him how I feel–that I think he's a great back but wish he wouldn't down my abilities because it's really unnecessary and it's not beneficial to either of us. I think we could be friends if we sat down and talked."

I do think Taylor is a terrific fullback. It is all the more to his credit that he has become one without possessing exceptional gifts. If I had Aladdin's lamp I would ask the jinni to give me Buddy Dial's hands, Bobby Mitchell's moves, Lenny Moore's change of pace. But Jim Taylor has no gift that I would want. He became an outstanding back because of sheer determination, which speaks as well for a football player as anything possibly could. He hustles. He has worked on his balance, he has built up his strength. He has refined his philosophy of running. It used to be said of him that he would actually seek out tacklers for the sheer joy of trying to run over them, but now he realizes that by skirting around tacklers you can go a longer way. In short, he is mighty dangerous.

My point, however, is that he needn't feel Jim Brown has to be a bum in order for Jim Taylor to be a star. In 1962 he outrushed me. He gained 1474 yards while I dropped off to 996. Now that was a tremendous performance he gave, and it would have been just as tremendous even if I had gained two thousand yards that year. There is room for both of us at the bank.

People tell me, "If you had Green Bay's offensive line in front of you, there's no telling how many yards you'd gain." I don't buy that. The Packer line is considered the best blocking line in the league, yet it is possible I might gain fewer yards running behind the Packers than I do behind my own Cleveland line. My line and I work well together. That is an established fact. While on the other hand, there is no guarantee that I would fit in as well behind the Packer line. When a back starts telling himself that he could be better than a rival back if he only had that guy's line, he's in trouble.

Without trying to be the least bit falsely modest, I must say that some of my boosters have overrated me. This is not to deny that I find it heartwarming to read that so fine a linebacker as ex-Eagle Chuck Bednarik has said of me, "He's superhuman. . . . You can forget your Nagurskis and Jim Thorpes. I'll take Jimmy Brown." Nor is it to deny that it ruffles me to have a magazine state that "no other fullback starts faster [than Jim Taylor], not even the swifter Jim Brown, who needs running room to get up his full head of steam." Knowing that I once beat Olympic sprinter Paul Drayton in four consecutive getaway sprints of ten, twenty, thirty, and forty yards, I must question that I need "running room." (Of course, Paul is still after me for a rematch, claiming he was out of condition, but I've told him I have retired undefeated.) Yet while knowing my pluses and taking pride in them, I also know full well that I've seen ball carriers who could do things on a football field that I can never hope to master. For instance, when it comes to pure grace, I have seen no one come close to Hugh McElhenny.

In his prime The King had the prettiest moves, the most beautiful high step, the smoothest change of pace that you would ever hope to see. He may well have been the greatest screen-pass runner in history. In 1963, with the Giants, he was old and slow and heavy, but just to show he still had the fakes he faked two of our defensive backs flat on their faces and went in for a touchdown. The King was a genius who even in old age added class to the title-winning Giants.

As a long-gain threat I am not even in the same class with Bobby Mitchell, a halfback with Cleveland but now a flanker with Washington. To my mind, he is the greatest breakaway threat in football. When he played for the Browns we roomed together, and yet I must tell Bobby that I suspect he has not tapped his full potential.

He is not a loafer by any means, but I would like to see him adopt a conditioning program that would make his innards scream. In 1963 I worked harder in preseason camp than I ever had, and as a result I had my best season. Consequently it is my hunch that if Bobby Mitchell, with his unique breakaway talent, conditioned himself beyond the normal expectations he could be the one man in football capable of playing flanker and half-back and returning punts and kickoffs. He would either tear the league apart or keel over. The rewards are worth the gamble.

Baltimore's Lenny Moore is another back with a talent I envy. He has a little change-of-pace dip motion that has made monkeys out of tacklers. I first caught a glimpse of it when I was a sophomore cornerback in the Syracuse defense and Lenny was a junior halfback at Penn State.

"This guy's tough," I was told a few days before the game by Roy Simmons, one of our coaches. "When he swings around the end don't look at his legs. Don't try to tackle his legs. Just put your eyes on his belt buckle and keep them there and hit him fairly high–up around his middle. Otherwise he's going to give you a leg and then take it away so fast you won't know where it went."

"Right, coach," I said.

Going into the game, I reminded myself to do what Coach Simmons had told me. The first time Lenny Moore came around end he gave me that little dip. It came a little early, before I was close enough to make contact, but I still held good field position on Lenny and was moving with him as he swung toward the sideline after giving me the dip. Now I was ready to drive on him. I flew at him. But I was just a shade low—down at his thighs instead of at his belt. Dip! His legs were in and out and gone. And then, whoosh, the burst of speed. By the time I looked around he'd gone about twenty-seven yards for a touchdown.

Well, a ballplayer can marvel at the Lenny Moore dip, the McElhenny grace, the Mitchell broken-field run, but in the end, corny as it may sound, you know you have to be lucky as well as good. I think of John David Crow, the St. Louis fullback whose tremendous ability has been canceled out by injuries . . . or of Ollie Matson, a fullback fast enough to win Olympic medals but one who at the peak of his career fell into the hands of a Los Angeles club that saw fit to make him a defensive safety.

I have been luckier than the Crows and Matsons. But lest I overdo the humility bit, I'll close my observations on opponents I have known with a small story that falls under the heading of Patting Myself on the Back. The opponent in this case was a linebacker named Sam Valentine, who played for Penn State at the time I played for Syracuse.

The week before our two teams were to meet, one of the Penn State coaches, Joe Paterno, gave Valentine special instructions for dealing with me. Paterno had heard through the grapevine that tacklers could discourage me by consistently hitting me with all their might, even when I didn't have the ball. He was skeptical of the story, but decided to use it for whatever it might be worth. So he went to Sam Valentine figuring that he at least would put Valentine in a winning frame of mind.

"Hit Brown hard on every play, whether he has the ball or not," Paterno told him. "He doesn't stand up well under a beating. After a while he'll start dogging it."

Every time Valentine could reach me in the first half he

slammed into me as hard as he could. But I was having a pretty fair day. In the Penn State dressing room at halftime, Valentine said to Joe Paterno:

"Hey, coach. You know what you told me about Brown?"

"Yeh, what about it?" said Paterno.

"Well, I did exactly what you told me. I hit him hard every play, and you know what?"

"What?"

"Coach," said Valentine, "you're a goddammed liar."

CHAPTER 4

Does Brown block?

There is a sports columnist named Larry Merchant who works for the Philadelphia *Daily News*. During the 1963 football season he hit upon a theme that captured his fancy, and proceeded to devote a considerable amount of newsprint to it. His message was that I do not choose to block.

His first attack on my blocking—or is it non-blocking?—was headlined:

GREAT, GREAT RUN—BUT NO BLOCK

Proceeding from there, Merchant began:

"One of the intriguing paradoxes in the world of fun and games is that Jim Brown is the greatest runner in the history of football—and one of its worst blockers.

"There is irony in this because he led the revolt that overthrew Paul Brown 'for the good of the team,' yet he refuses to do something very basic for the good of the team; because it is quite obvious that he could block as well as he chose to, which means he doesn't choose to; and because, nevertheless, he is beyond any question the spiritual and physical leader of the Cleveland Browns.

"In a perverse way this is a remarkable tribute to Brown's unmatched ability as a ball carrier. . . . Nobody seems even to care if he blocks or not."

Having flattered me to the extent of crediting me with the power, magnetism, and political agility to lead forty adult men in revolt against their coach, Merchant went on to further invest in me the capacity to terrorize my teammates into a state of speechlessness. He wrote, "The Browns, whose destiny is tied to Brown and who are as awed by his ball-carrying as you and I, either cover up for him by denying the obvious or simply won't discuss it."

In short, Larry Merchant, who is a hard-working and entertaining writer and one who has had a little experience playing and coaching football, charged me with neglecting an important duty and thereby demeaning my own record.

Actually, I was well aware that my role as a blocker, such as it is, had long been a subject of player conversation throughout the league. I was not mad at anyone who said I could not, or would not, block. At a time when there was no provocation for me to discuss the matter, I brought it up on my Cleveland TV show, simply because I thought it might interest the fans.

Perhaps I am not as good a blocker as I ought to be. I will not be the judge of that. I will readily concede that I am not as good a blocker as I could be if I concentrated more on blocking. There are reasons why I don't.

First of all, though, I must expect to have my blocking criticized. When a ballplayer is supposed to be "great, great"—Merchant used the words, I didn't—he is then analyzed from top to bottom. Frequently his strong points are praised and exaggerated out of due proportion and his weak points are made to appear weaker than they are. That is part of the game, I suppose.

Anyhow, the main reason that I don't concentrate on my blocking is that under Cleveland's offensive system I am called upon to block very seldom. I didn't design the system, but frankly, I like it that way.

In our system I do most of the running. In '63, for example, I ran more than any back in the league. I was the ball carrier on more than 63 percent of Cleveland's ground plays. Even that statistic does not alone cover my running game, for the Browns throw a good many short passes to me in the flat and these are basically running plays, not pass plays.

In most cases when our halfback runs I am supposed to be a decoy, not a blocker. When we pass I am usually supposed to flare out as a safety-valve receiver or as a screen-pass or swing-pass receiver. (In the safety-valve role, I frequently am not thrown to, so critics of my blocking are given an excellent opportunity to say, "Look at Brown, will you? He's just standing there doing nothing.") When a play calls for double protection, I block for the passer. I have experienced satisfaction from throwing good blocks. If our coaching staff decided to enlarge my blocking role, I would get out on the practice field with John Wooten and Gene Hickerson, our guards, and try to learn all of their techniques. I would be in my room at night going through the motions. As it is, I am in my room going through the motions of running. The pressure is on me to run. My running constitutes my principal value to the team. When I fail to gain a hundred yards in a game, people say that I had a poor day. The fact is, if I went through an entire season gaining ninety-eight yards in every game, some of the same people who call me a poor blocker would be the first to announce that I was washed up as a runner. At season's end, of course, they would find that I had gained 1372 yards, which calls for a raise in any league. But they would have spent most of the season wondering if I had grown old. So as long as our coaches ask no more than an occasional block from me, I am going to continue to devote all my attention to running.

When I say there is pressure on me to run, I mean just that. For example, I was criticized for poor blocking—and my blocking *was* poor—in a game last year at New York. The fact was, however, that it was practically impossible for me to block. For one thing, I had water on the elbow that gave me considerable pain with every contact. (After the game my arm was so swollen that I had trouble putting on my shirt.) Secondly, I was trying to make out the New York Giants through blurred vision.

The Giants had started out giving my face a pounding. Ever since the first quarter I could see players only as one might see a man on the opposite side of a light curtain.

In any case, the point is that the pressure was on me to stay in that game and keep running. I did not mention my blurred vision to my teammates or coaches, nor have I spoken of it until now. My silence constituted no act of bravery. I ask no medals. Linemen go on playing with broken ribs, and by the same token I was simply doing what I am paid to do, and by that I mean keep running as long as it is possible to run effectively. I could make out the shadowy tacklers well enough to try to run away from them, and when necessary, over them. My legs were strong and my mind was clear. With the help of the players who *do* the blocking in the Cleveland system, I was able to run thirty-two yards for a touchdown. And when quarterback Frank Ryan put a short swing pass right into my hands I was able to run seventy-two yards for another touchdown, again behind the men who do the blocking. I carried the ball twenty-three times and caught four shorty passes that Ryan plopped into my hands.

We won, 35–24. My teammates did not ask me why I hadn't blocked. They simply gave me the game ball. I doubt that players vote game balls to men who shirk their jobs.

In any event, although I am asked to block on only a small fraction of our plays, I think that if an objective study were made of the blocks I do throw, a few people might be pleasantly surprised with the results. I may not blast linemen off their feet, but I believe I usually get sufficiently in their way to keep them away from the passer. I'm glad that I'm not asked to block more than a few times a game. It's a matter of football economics. If I were a majority blocker rather than a majority runner, I would not receive the salary I get. There are more good blockers than good runners. As a matter of fact, it is kind of curious that most backfield men who can't run very well always seem to be good blockers. "My guy's a helluva blocker," says the coach who has been unable to negotiate a trade for a running threat. A close look around the league will turn up, I think, a number of good blockers who were once fine runners but have grown old. This can best be explained, perhaps, in terms of my own plans for the future. If, when I have slowed and gone over the hill, I find that I want to hang onto my football job, I shall get out there on the practice field and work long and hard with those guards and become a great, great blocker.

CHAPTER 5

1963—A new deal

Looking back on the 1963 football season, my most recent as this is written, my mind pokes around as one would in a large house of many rooms. There is nothing if not variety and a sense of never having been in such a place. Some of the rooms I don't care for. But I come away feeling, on the whole, very pleased.

The '63 season was, of course, the first I spent–the first the Cleveland Browns spent–under a head coach other than Paul Brown. It was a time of rising hopes–six victories in our first six games. A time of disappointment–four defeats in our last eight games. It was a time of personal achievement when I ran for a record-breaking 1863 yards, and yet if there was one play alone that reversed our rush toward the championship, that play was one I botched.

The 1963 season was a happy time. I had freedom to run in any direction and I was on a club that had an esprit de corps. Yet '63 was a season in which I came to realize that I could lose my eyesight playing this game and that I was going to have to fight to see that this didn't happen.

We had a chance to win the title right up to the next-to-last game of the season, but when it was all over we finished second. Still, our 10–4 record was the best, percentagewise, that a Cleveland squad had registered in four years. For a team rebuilding, that wasn't bad.

All told, 1963 was the most thoroughly enjoyable season of my professional career.

We liked our new coach, Blanton Collier, and yet at first we resisted him. Our resistance was not active or even conscious, yet it was a problem he had to overcome. When we first reported to training camp, Blanton delivered a talk. As mild and polite as he is, he can become quite excited when he addresses a squad. He speaks faster and faster as he gets carried away. And now you could feel an undercurrent of his excitement when he first spoke to us. The gist of what he said was this:

"Participation is what I want here. In other words, I want to see you men taking on responsibility. For one thing, I'm open to suggestions. All the coaches are open to suggestions. If you have an idea for a play, or if you have an idea that will improve a play, tell us. I won't guarantee we'll use your idea, but we'll listen.

"We're all in this together. We'll get nowhere if a man feels he's won a victory by putting something over on a coach. Another thing. This club has been too quiet. Let's hear some noise on that bench. Help each other out, whether it's in practice or in a game or wherever. If it's only a matter of a guy coming off the field and needing a towel, get him a towel. The whole point is that we want a lot of participation—we don't want a collection of men who are satisfied to go through their own little routine and then call it a day."

This was the kind of speech I enjoyed hearing. It was, I thought, much better than listening to Paul Brown tell us he would fine us without hesitation or that he expected us to have civilized table manners.

Yet our club did not immediately respond to Blanton's new deal. Having silently taken orders from Paul, we had more or less been in a shell and it wasn't easy to come out. The training camp looked no different now—the dormitory rooms were the same, the field was the same, our practice schedule was roughly the same. With the exception of Dub Jones, our new end coach, there were no new faces on the coaching staff. Blanton made curfew a half-hour later—ten-thirty instead of ten—but that alone wasn't enough to loosen us up. We did not rush to the coaches with suggestions. The feeling that existed was still, "Well, coach, it's your play. All we do is run it."

Personalities don't change overnight. Under Paul, we'd acted like business executives. Whenever a play clicked, we didn't walk around smiling. Be calm—that was our motto. Go on to the next play. But then, gradually, we responded to Blanton's call for noise. We caught a whiff of new zest in the air. For example, Fritzie Heisler, who had first coached under Paul Brown at Massillon High School in 1938, seemed a new man. Runty and bespectacled, he looks more like a pawnbroker than a line coach, but Blanton calls him the best in the business, and now Fritzie was working and meeting with our linemen with the enthusiasm of a kid who had found a new toy. Those linemen weren't getting much time for lunch.

Blanton himself, though, did more than anyone to sell us.

He won over John Wooten fast. During a practice session, Blanton had called attention to one of our guards who had just let a defensive lineman run him into the backfield. Wooten, a guard himself, spoke up, telling Blanton that on the particular play we had just run it was next to impossible to handle a man who charged low. "He gets under you and raises you up every time," said Wooten. "A guard's helpless on this play." Under Paul Brown, Wooten would have kept his mouth shut.

"You can handle him," Blanton replied, "if you pick out one spot on him—maybe his right knee, or anything else. Just pick out a target and keep your eye on that spot and drive your shoulder into it regardless of where that spot goes. That man will not get under you."

Two days later I was sitting in the locker room when Wooten came in. "You know that block Blanton was showing me the other day?" he said. "I'll be doggoned if it doesn't work. I've been trying it on Kanicki all day. It's such a small thing, but it's a helluva thing."

Veterans with secure jobs began to look like college kids trying to make the varsity. Guard Gene Hickerson and I both have a tendency to appear lazy because we are big, lumbering men. But Hickerson trained like a madman under the new deal, and I ran series after series of 330-yard sprints.

We were catching the spirit that Blanton had asked of us, and as soon as the exhibition schedule began we saw that even though he was on the spot as Paul's successor he was not going to be the kind of guy who might panic. Anxious to give every player a careful look, he laid out a plan for substituting by quarters and stuck to it regardless of how bad it made him look in the eyes of the fans. We lost to Detroit and then, before a huge doubleheader crowd in Cleveland, lost to Baltimore. We had a strong drive going against the Colts but Blanton broke it up at the quarter by sending in a new center, a rookie flanker, a sophomore guard, and another guard we had just picked up in a trade. We knew then that Blanton really meant to know his personnel and find his best players.

The next week we went to San Francisco and whacked the 49ers as hard as we could because we realized that Art Modell needed a win for the season ticket sales. Then we beat the Rams but closed out the exhibition schedule with a rotten performance against Pittsburgh.

"Bring back Paul Brown!" the fans cried.

Nuts. I knew by now we had a contender, and I said so. I for one wasn't going to burn myself out in an exhibition game a week before the league opener.

So far as player personnel was concerned, our main problem was to rebuild. Mike McCormack, our captain and offensive tackle, had made up his mind to retire. Flanker Ray Renfro was nearing the end of the trail. We hadn't yet regained the ground that we had lost on the trade that sent Bobby Mitchell and a first draft choice to Washington for Ernie Davis. Not only was Ernie dead but so was Don Fleming, a brilliant defensive back who had been electrocuted while doing construction work in June. In short, we were going to depend heavily on relatively inexperienced men. Frank Ryan would be a full-time quarterback for the first time in his career. Halfback Ernie Green, with only one season of experience, was in the same boat. We needed a new "money" pass-catcher–a guy who could make the clutch catch–and the coaches picked Gary Collins, another who had only one season under his belt.

Maybe we were a little green but that didn't worry us, for the coaches had gotten us to think positively. The conservatism of past years was thrown out the window. Blanton decided to begin every game with a daring play. We were not going to run into the middle of the line for a yard so we could feel out our opponents. We wanted yardage at once, and when we rode through those first six league victories we usually got it.

The day before our first league game–against Washington–I dropped by the Browns office to pick up a few tickets and stopped in Art Modell's office to chat. "I can't overestimate the importance of this first game, Jim," Art told me. "It's just as big as can be." He did not have to explain. I knew what he was talking about. If we didn't come through, the wolves would be on him for having let Paul go. And I knew he meant the game was a big one for me, too, because I'd said publicly that I was glad to be rid of Paul.

I had a huge day. Yet it was just one play that occurred in the second quarter that told me times had changed. I caught a screen pass and bounced off several tacklers and went eighty-three yards for a touchdown. I was dumfounded to see practically our whole offensive unit follow me downfield to congratulate me. Our entire bench got up to greet me. There was not an ounce of phoniness in this exhibition of camaraderie. Those guys were just completely happy. Their happiness gave me a big lift, and it seemed that everyone now realized for a certainty that we were going to be a team to be reckoned with. After the game, Art Modell came into the dressing room and said to me:

"Thank you, Jim. Thanks very much."

I was touched. Clubowners do not ordinarily hustle downstairs to say thanks. Art had given me a square shot, and just knowing my big day meant so much to him gave me a tremendous feeling inside.

Every day you could see the results of Blanton's plea that we pull together and help each other. Off in a corner of the practice field you could see Paul Wiggin, a veteran defensive tackle, sweating to get young John Brown ready for his forthcoming meeting with strongman Bob Lilly of the Dallas Cowboys. We worried about Lilly.

He is a defensive end with cute moves. John Brown, as the offensive tackle who would play opposite him, knew Lilly's strategy. Lilly grabs the tackle, then tries to go outside him. And when the tackle starts overplaying to the outside Lilly snatches him across his body and cuts back inside. Defensive men are allowed to grab jerseys, so John Brown knew that one of the most difficult parts of his job would be to keep knocking Lilly's hands off him. Paul Wiggin played the role of Bob Lilly off in that corner of the field and really shaped up John, who went out and played a fine game against Lilly.

Blanton's new deal was complete. The previous year Paul Brown had told us we would have to play a throwing game against Dallas—that the Dallas defense was too tough to run against. As a runner, I had been particularly infuriated by Paul's strategy. I am convinced that there is no team in football you can't run against.

Under Blanton now, we mixed up our plays—we ran and we

passed—and I found I could run against Dallas to the extent of 232 yards. In one hundred-degree Texas temperature we knocked off the team *Sports Illustrated* football writer Tex Maule had picked to win the title. Even in the closing minutes, with a 41–24 victory locked up, there was fresh evidence of the good feeling and consideration that every man in our organization had for the next. Dub Jones phoned down from his booth and told Blanton:

"Get Jim back into the game. He needs only six yards to break his own single-game rushing record."

Blanton could not send me in, simply because Dallas kept the ball the rest of the game. I didn't care much about the record; actually, I was pooped and had no urge to run again in that Texas sun. But the fact that Dub and Blanton and our players wanted me to break the record was important to me.

Frank Ryan, meanwhile, was standing up beautifully as our quarterback. A mathematician studying for his Ph.D., he went at the job of quarterbacking as methodically as if he were writing a paper on physics. He was icily calm; he spoke in a whisper. "Look," I'd tell him in the huddle, "this play is not going to work. Don't change the tempo here." and Ryan would say in that whispering voice of his:

"Okay, okay. Take it easy now, Jim. Just take it easy."

Ryan was as fearless as any quarterback in the league. In fact, I considered him slightly crazy. I doubted that he was capable of feeling pain. Though frail and a bleeder, he would stand out there with blood pouring from his nose, and for all I could tell, he didn't even know he was bleeding. He wouldn't even wipe the blood away.

In one game our strategy called for running out the clock toward the end of the first half. I figured Ryan would give me the ball for line smashes. But in the huddle he announced he would keep the ball and try to run laterally behind the line of scrimmage. Now that is a very good way for a quarterback to be broken in half by linemen who like nothing better than a chance to cripple a quarterback, and so I said to Ryan:

"Are you out of your mind?"

"No," he whispered. "I've gotta protect you from injury, Jim."

"You've gotta protect *me?"*

I held my breath while I watched him run out the clock.

Blanton's invitation to us to suggest plays paid off. Our fourth game, in Cleveland, was a battle for first place. The Pittsburgh Gas House Gang came to town riding high, boasting the best defensive statistics in the league. In practice a few days before the game, we were working on a short-yardage play—a simple dive play in which I smash over right guard. It's a logical play used when a yard is needed for a first down. But suddenly Frank Ryan said to Blanton:

"They'll be playing Jim hard on this play. They'll be looking for him. Now if we use the play once or twice and get in a situation where they'll be looking for it again, why don't I fake to Jim and then go off tackle or around end? I think I can get through for good yardage."

"Sounds logical," said Blanton. We hashed over the play in a meeting. Should we change the blocking in order to give Ryan the best possible hole? "No," said Ryan. "If we change the blocking we may tip off Pittsburgh that something's new. This has got to be a surprise play." On Ryan's surprise play he rode into the line behind me, slipped around me, and ran thirteen yards for a touchdown.

The largest crowd in Cleveland's football history—an 84,684 sellout—packed the stadium for the Pittsburgh game. Ed Brown, the Steeler quarterback, turned up throwing like a Sammy Baugh. "Is this guy ever going to miss?" we asked ourselves. But our defense twice held the Steelers on our one-yard line and sparked our offense into a fourth-quarter rally that gave us a 35–23 victory. The nice part about winning was that we had been able to run our best plays without having to sell our coaches on them. At halftime I said to Howard Brinker: "Let's ditch the 15 play. They're penetrating on me before I can get up to the line."

Howard was not compelled to give Blanton a longwinded explanation of why we ought to ditch the 15 play, as he had had to do under Paul Brown. Howard put an 18-19 regular on the blackboard for the second half, but I said, "I can't run that sweep because their ends are playing us wide and our halfback won't be able to get to them with a block. How about an 18-S or an 18-toss?" The 18-S would pull a tackle out of the line to block, and the 18-toss would send our slot end after their defensive end with a perfect blocking angle on him.

"Good enough," was the answer I got. I am not trying to picture myself as a tactical genius or as an unofficial assistant coach—we were simply going on the theory that forty heads are better than half a dozen. Players see things on the field that coaches sometimes miss.

Anyhow, we beat Pittsburgh, and long after the game had ended I emerged from the dressing room and was startled by the sight that confronted me. There under the stands stood several hundred fans, packed shoulder to shoulder. They did not shout congratulations or clamor for autographs. They stood there in silence. I had the feeling that this was their way of saying, "Thanks for a good performance. We thought we'd wait around to tell you we liked it." This was one of the most moving moments I have known in football.

The Browns were flying. We were loose. Our attitude going into each game was hustle hard and let the chips fall where they may. Ryan's passes were true, and his receivers snatched them as nonchalantly as kids shagging flies. I had never known such fun. I slept and ate football. I would be driving my car and suddenly slap the wheel excitedly. In my mind's eye I could see a big hole opening up in the line and feel myself roaring through it. It's a wonder I didn't knock off a pedestrian.

The week after the Steeler game, we went into New York for

the big test against the Eastern champion Giants. We beat them, 35–24, but that game was one of the roughest that I have ever played. My vision was blurred for about 80 percent of the game. Although I made no mention of this fact to players or press, this is as good a place as any, I suppose, to disclose what happened and to serve notice that I do not intend to have it happen again.

The Giants pounded my eyes unmercifully with forearms and elbows. At least seven times they dug through over my face bar.

So far as I know, only one man suspected I couldn't see well. "Are you all right?" one of the officials asked me. "I'm okay," I told him. I kept blinking, trying to get clear vision to return but nothing helped. The next day the newspapers carried a U.P.I. photo showing me sitting on the bench covering my eyes with one hand; the photo was captioned "Moment of Meditation." I was not, of course, meditating.

Yet as I have said, I am paid to stay in there and run, and inasmuch as my head was clear I saw no reason to beg off. Nor did I complain about the Giants' tactics. To this day I hold no animosity toward them. I mean, let's face it, I have to expect the opposition to pay special attention to me, and I don't blame them for going as far as they can possibly go undetected.

After the game I went straight to my hotel room and lay down. The next morning my sight was no better, but I went to Leone's restaurant to speak at the weekly luncheon of New York's Monday Quarterback Club. A mouse under one of my eyes prompted considerable discussion of the rough treatment that I had received but I tried to make a joke out of it. I spotted good old Sam Huff in the audience and, with a slight dig at Jim Taylor and his anti-Huff accusations, told the Monday Quarterbacks: "I hold Sam Huff's future in my hand."

The luncheon was full of good-humored banter. Toastmaster Kyle Rote said, "I want to thank Jim for having us for lunch—for the second day in a row." I shook hands all around—with Rote, with Huff, with other Giants—and flew back to Cleveland, thinking my sight would soon clear up. When it did not by midweek, I went to see an eye specialist. He took X-rays and treated me with drops and was vague when I asked him how serious my condition was. By the time I got home I had arrived at a decision that put football in its proper perspective. I was mad. I said to myself: "The hell with this. I'm not going to sacrifice my eyesight for football. I'm not going to let anyone mess around with my face any more. If it means I'll have to fight and get thrown out of the game, okay, but nobody is taking shots at my eyes from here in."

I had never been in a football fight. As I have said, my theory is that I am better off not letting my opponents know when they get under my skin. So I psyche them with a poker face. But when it comes to risking your eyesight, it's no time for psyching. A broken bone is one thing, but blindness is another. Jeopardize my sight and I'll kick your teeth in.

My vision was still somewhat blurred when, following our New York victory, we took on the Philadelphia Eagles in Cleveland. But I wasn't the only one who'd come out of that New York rumble a little the worse for wear. Ten of our men had had to lay out of practice, and three of them–defensive men Galen Fiss, Mike Lucci, and Jim Shofner–had to sit out the Eagles game. Yet we ripped the Eagles apart, 37–7, prompting Blanton Collier to say of us, "They've got the doggondest spirit and attitude I've ever seen in all my years in football."

Ironically, it was immediately after Blanton spoke that we began to lose the attitude that had carried us this far. Undefeated in six games, we had set a fantastic pace. We were whipping through a league that was supposed to be too tough to steamroll. The press raved. Cleveland fans clamored at the box-office for standing-room tickets. On all sides we were pronounced a great football team, and the only question was, how great? "This is one of the greatest Browns teams of all times," ex-Brown Tony Adamle told columnist Frank Gibbons.

And so our success became our undoing. The fact was, we were in many respects, at many positions, a young team. We had been playing our games one at a time, as the saying goes, and having a ball. Now, suddenly, like a man who wakes up one morning and finds himself President, we became aware of our position. We were on top, so we were supposed to stay on top. We were being called great, so if we failed to win the championship we would be bums. *The Saturday Evening Post* headlined a story "Team on Trial"—an ultimatum to us to win the title or admit that we had been guilty of stupidity in cheering Paul Brown's departure.

So we became obsessed with the league standings. Players—particularly the younger ones, I believe—began looking weeks ahead, trying to figure how many Cleveland wins and how many New York and St. Louis and Pittsburgh losses it would take to give us the title. Fatheadedness was not our problem. Our problem, as we were to learn, was caution. "We can't make a mistake now," the feeling went, "because we really have a shot at the big prize."

The Giants were coming to town for a rematch. Looking back, I am convinced that if we had whacked the Giants again we would have regained our looseness. But they whacked us, and yours truly takes the blame.

In practice we worked on the play we would use the first time we got the ball. Once again, we hoped to start in a positive fashion, to hit the opponent with a big play at the outset. The play was designed to spring me loose. It was a fake sweep around right end. It was set up perfectly. I would take two steps to my right as if fixing to sweep. One guard would pull out of the line and another would trap, again indicating a sweep. Frank Ryan would fake a quick pitchout to me, but abruptly I would pivot and shoot for the middle and Ryan would slam the ball into my belly. The idea was to get that Giant line moving for the sweep—to get middle linebacker Sam Huff flowing out of his position and then hit right over it. The chances were good that they would fall for the scheme, for this season I had been running outside more than ever in my career.

We received the opening kickoff and then lined up for the play that we had worked so hard to perfect. As I took my stance I said to myself:

"Now don't fumble, don't fumble. Make sure you get this run off."

The play worked beautifully. The Giants bit like a kid digging into a watermelon. Huff jerked out of his area and left a gaping hole. It was the kind of hole you just pour through so fast that your speedometer zings to full-out. You have so much daylight that you practically *know* you can outmaneuver those defensive backs and go all the way.

Carrying the ball in my right hand, I roared into that hole, but just as I got there the damndest accident happened. To my left, John Morrow, our center, had a good block on huge Giant tackle John LoVetere. Unable to get past Morrow, LoVetere spun off him like a top, pivoting backwards and away from the play. With his back to me, LoVetere could not even know where I was. But as he spun in a half-circle, the back of his outstretched right hand knocked the ball out of my hand. Huff, faked out of position, found himself lying on the football.

The Giants kicked a field goal, then turned right around and intercepted a Ryan pass and got a quick touchdown, and with less than three minutes gone had a 10–0 lead. Whereas I might have given us a one-touchdown lead on the first play and convinced our players that we were going to rack up the Giants, we now became a mistake-conscious team. We tightened up.

Y. A. Tittle picked us to pieces with short passes. One reason the Giants won the Eastern title in 1961, '62, and '63 is that they are intelligent players–they play intelligent defense, they help each other out, they hold their opponents in high regard. But without Tittle, they are just another team. He's fiery; he slams his helmet to the ground, he chews out his players, he even snaps at himself. But players work for him, knowing he can deliver because he sets up for a pass and releases the ball sidearm with phenomenal speed. In my early years of pro ball I regarded Norm Van Brocklin as the best quarterback in the business, and then I swung over to Johnny Unitas, but now I have to go with Tittle. We knew he meant to riddle our intermediate zone, but being tense, we were helpless.

Slaughtering us, the Giants had no need to batter me that day. We had the ball so little that I carried only nine times. In the last minute of play, however, Giant linebacker Tom Scott clubbed me in the eye with a forearm. I slugged him, he came back swinging, and we both were out of the game. I am not mad at Scott. As I've said, anyone is welcome to try anything he likes, but nobody's going to endanger my eyesight without getting a fight.

Anyhow, we had been beaten, 33–6, and we began to doubt ourselves. Our veterans knew that one lousy game means nothing, but you could see Ryan and the others who were getting their first big shot losing their abandon.

Blanton Collier attacked the problem objectively, working hard to correct the new faults that now cropped up in execution. But we were psychologically doomed. When the Detroit Lions finally knocked us out of the race, it was like looking at an old photograph and seeing yourself as you once were. The Lions, with nothing at stake, were loose.

As this book is written, I have no predictions to offer—I do not predict the Browns will win titles. The league is tough. But I believe our players now realize that it does no good to let one rotten game nag them, or to project ahead and try to calculate the standings, or to concern themselves with living up to press clippings. It is up to us to profit from our 1963 experience.

It was, again, a season I enjoyed more thoroughly than any. I played my best because I was allowed to play my best—not because I wanted to show up Paul Brown. I have stated that he was a great coach who once again can become a great coach if he bends just an inch or two. After the '63 season ended I was glad to note that Larry Merchant, my articulate critic of the Philadelphia press who had acidly dubbed me Coach Jimmy Brown and then taken to booming Paul for the head coaching vacancy in Philadelphia, agreed with me precisely.

"Can Brown handle the Eagles?" asked Merchant. "Are his imperious ways outdated in getting the most out of players? This remains to be seen. What must be remembered is that he is an extremely intelligent fellow. He can't change his nature, but he can modify it. It is not far-fetched to conjecture that his enforced vacation of a year has been cathartic, that it may have freshened his spirit, sharpened his focus, regenerated his enthusiasm, providing a climate for re-evaluation."

I could not have put it better, or even as well.

I wish Paul success. As for myself, I can only say that football once again is fun. At twenty-eight, I have a lot more fun ahead of me.

Index